T0079224

Praise for
WHAT THE DOG KNOWS
Young Readers Edition

"*What the Dog Knows* offers a fascinating, fun glimpse into the world of dogs. If you've ever loved a dog, you will adore this book."

—Robert Crais, *New York Times* bestselling mystery author
of *Suspect* and *The Wanted*

"Learn about the fascinating world of training working dogs to identify scents, rescue people, find explosives, and assist law enforcement."

—Temple Grandin, *New York Times* bestselling author
of *Animals in Translation* and *Animals Make Us Human*

"Cat Warren's tale of how she turned her unruly puppy into a happy working-dog partner—by following his nose—is a great dog story. *What the Dog Knows* is far more uplifting than any book featuring human cadavers, regular tick sightings, and travels through poison ivy has any right to be. Go find it!"

—Alexandra Horowitz, author
of *Inside of a Dog—Young Readers Edition: What Dogs See, Smell, and Know*

"I'd like to shake Solo's paw for inspiring this super-interesting, fun book about how four-legged heroes work. It's a must-read for anyone who wants to know more about how our best friends work (and play)."

—Maria Goodavage, *New York Times* bestselling author
of *Top Dog: The Story of Marine Hero Lucca*

"Cat Warren has taken her original book—destined to become a classic—and reimagined it for young readers. Beautifully illustrated, *What the Dog Knows* is perfect for young minds who will embrace the almost magical world of dogs and scent detection. A must for animal lovers and budding researchers."

—Brian Hare and Vanessa Woods, *New York Times* bestselling authors
of *The Genius of Dogs*

WHAT THE DOG KNOWS

Young Readers Edition

written by

CAT WARREN

ILLUSTRATIONS BY PATRICIA J. WYNNE

Simon & Schuster Books for Young Readers

New York   London   Toronto   Sydney   New Delhi

For David and the dogs

SIMON & SCHUSTER BOOKS FOR YOUNG READERS
An imprint of Simon & Schuster Children's Publishing Division
1230 Avenue of the Americas, New York, New York 10020
Text copyright © 2013, 2019 by Cat Warren
Jacket photographs copyright © 2019 by iStock
Interior illustrations copyright © 2019 by Patricia J. Wynne
All rights reserved, including the right of
reproduction in whole or in part in any form.
SIMON & SCHUSTER BOOKS FOR YOUNG READERS
is a trademark of Simon & Schuster, Inc.
For information about special discounts for bulk purchases,
please contact Simon & Schuster Special Sales at
1-866-506-1949 or business@simonandschuster.com.
The Simon & Schuster Speakers Bureau can bring authors to
your live event. For more information or to book an event, contact
the Simon & Schuster Speakers Bureau at 1-866-248-3049
or visit our website at www.simonspeakers.com.
Jacket design by Lucy Ruth Cummins
Interior design by Tom Daly
The text for this book was set in Excelsior LT Std.
The illustrations for this book were rendered in pen and ink.
Manufactured in the United States of America
0919 FFG
First Edition
10 9 8 7 6 5 4 3 2 1
Library of Congress Cataloging-in-Publication Data
Names: Warren, Cat, author.
Title: What the dog knows : scent, science,
and the amazing ways dogs perceive the world / Cat Warren.
Description: Young reader's edition. | First edition. | New York : Simon & Schuster
Books for Young Readers, [2019] | Audience: Age 8-12. | Audience: Grade 4 to 6. |
Includes bibliographical references.
Identifiers: LCCN 2018055766 |
ISBN 9781534428140 (hardcover : alk. paper) | ISBN 9781534428164 (eBook)
Subjects: LCSH: Tracking and trailing—Juvenile literature. | Tracking and trailing.
Classification: LCC SF428.75 .W37 2019 | DDC 636.7/0886—dc23
LC record available at https://lccn.loc.gov/2018055766

CONTENTS

● ● ● ● ● ● ● ● ●

CHAPTER ONE

• • • • • • • • • • • •

A FURRY PRINCE

The e-mail arrived in my inbox with a subject line that made my heart race: "Good News."

I had been waiting and hoping for nearly a year for a German shepherd pup from a respected breeder in Ohio. We wanted one of Joan's puppies. It seemed our wait was finally over.

"We have one gorgeous male," Joan said in her e-mail to me. But he had to be delivered by C-section, lifted out of his sedated mother's womb. He was a heavy lump. A litter of one.

I gazed at the photos Joan sent me with the lone male pup's birth announcement. In one shot he nestled in Joan's cupped hand. In another he was latched on to one of his mother's ten teats. Vita looked mournful, lying in the whelping box with one pup suckling.

No wonder he was strong. Inside the womb, he didn't have to share nourishment with other pups. Outside the womb, he had his choice of milk dispensers.

His head didn't look gorgeous. His nose looked squashed. His eyes were squinty. But I realized that Joan knew much more about newborn German shepherds than I did. This solitary pup was her twenty-fifth litter.

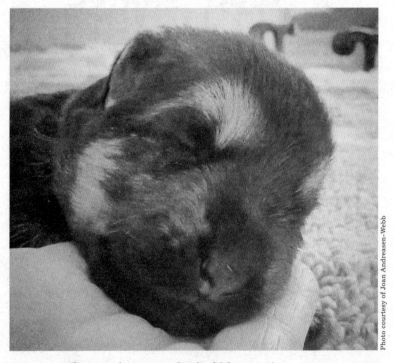

Photo courtesy of Joan Andreasen-Webb

The newborn pup looked like a mole to me.

The pup wasn't just handsome and strong, Joan told me. He also had a fine nose. The three of them had been back from the surgical delivery at the vet hospital for only a few hours, but when Joan walked into the room, the pup woke up and bobbled his head.

"His nose was working scent!" Joan wrote.

I read right past that piece of news. I knew what "working scent" meant, and it didn't interest me. I'd taught my German shepherds to keep their muzzles away from visitors' legs and crotches.

Dogs recognize each other that way. Most people find it rude.

"No sniff" was a standard command that David and I used in our house. But the house had been empty of German shepherds for nearly a year. Our sweet Zev had died almost a year earlier.

I found the most important news buried a few paragraphs down in Joan's e-mail: "You have the choice to have our little prince as we see how he develops." Then she assured me we could discuss any concerns I might have about his being "a singleton." She—along with her helpful adult shepherds—could help the pup overcome these issues.

Concerns? Absolutely not. David and I had a puppy! I had checked my e-mail every hour for the last week, waiting for news about the litter's arrival. Humans stay inside their mothers' wombs on average nine months from conception to birth. For dogs it's only about two months. But it felt so much longer to me.

Now it was early spring, and the next chapter of our life

with dogs could begin. This pup would play a starring role. I ran to find David, who was working on his logic classes in the study. "Puppy!" I said. He knew what I meant.

Then I flitted around the living room. I landed in front of my computer. My patient husband stood and listened as I read the entire e-mail to him.

I waited for my dizzy joy to ebb before responding to Joan. I wanted to sound like a grown-up. I was supposed to be one. I felt bad for her. All that planning and work and cost and hope. And one lone puppy instead of a squiggling mass of them. Other people who had been waiting for this day like me would be so disappointed.

I knew all of that. I also knew that we had the pup I wanted.

I had fallen in love with Joan's many German shepherds, and with the idea of this pup, ten months before. Joan lived in Ohio, but she bred and raised shepherds that had a West German family history.

As she weaned the pups from their mother's milk, she replaced it with goat milk and a raw-meat diet. They had lots of early exposure to woods and creeks, to friendly people and suburban malls, to toys and games—and to her other dogs.

Joan's adult dogs lay calmly on the sidewalk next to café tables. They attended children's reading hour at the library, heads planted between their paws, listening. They herded sheep, for fun. Some German shepherds, like border collies, have an innate desire to keep groups of people and animals together and moving in the right direction.

They also excelled in a sport called Schutzhund, a German word that means "protection dog." I didn't know much about it, except that the dogs had to bite someone on command. Luckily, that person had a hard protective sleeve on. A couple of Joan's pups grew up to become police K9s. When I was a newspaper reporter, I once spent the night shift with a patrol K9 and his handler. The dog's intensity and deep-throated bark startled me.

I didn't want that kind of German shepherd. This pup would have two jobs when he grew up. I wanted him to lie beneath my desk while I wrote articles and graded student papers, and then leap up and play ball in the yard with me when I wanted a break. If he won awards in the obedience ring, that would be a nice bonus.

I finally stopped daydreaming and looked up the word "singleton" on my computer. In math a singleton is a set with just one element. Most humans are singletons (though some of us are born as twins, or triplets). In dogs "singleton" means exactly the same thing, "a single one." But with horror stories attached.

The vast majority of puppies have littermates, from three to twelve, or more, depending on the breed. Those littermates exchange thousands of signals daily. That's part of how they grow and learn. They tumble over one another, squeaking and mewling at first, then, as their baby teeth come in, licking and biting, squealing in pain,

Solo was a singleton. Most pups have littermates who help them learn dog manners.

Solo photo by Sherri Clendenin
Litter photo by Diana Bunch

licking and wagging in apology. From there a pup might learn to bite a little less hard the second time.

Litters are adorable, and the puppies' interactions help each pup become a well-socialized dog. Pups learn to play well with others because they receive instant feedback from their littermates if they don't. That rough-and-tumble play can help a puppy learn how to deal with a variety of other dogs—the elderly miniature poodle in pain, the next-door neighbor's rude retriever. That play even prepares dogs for chance encounters with weird people.

As I kept reading, the tales of singletons got darker. A

singleton dog lives in a universe of "yes." A singleton tends to lack "bite inhibition" because he never learns from fellow pups what's too hard or what hurts. He doesn't know what a hard bite feels like. At the same time, a singleton can be overly sensitive to touch, even from his human. He's never had to sleep with a squirming or snoring littermate on top of him, or underneath him.

A singleton is "unable to get out of trouble calmly and graciously." (Although I wasn't an only child, I related to that one.) A single pup can have an "inability to handle frustration." (I related to that one too.)

I stopped reading about the bad and tried to focus on the good. Singleton dogs can sometimes make extraordinary companions, as they can bond closely with their people.

Sometimes.

. . . .

David and I avoided the nightmarish what-ifs that night. We wanted to celebrate. We had named this puppy even before Vita was pregnant with him. *Coda* means "tail" in Italian. A coda comes at the end of a long musical composition. A coda looks back, reflects, summarizes what came before.

This pup was going to run alongside us in the North Carolina woods near our home, be with us when we had dinner with friends. Sleep in our bedroom.

We were realistic. At least, we told ourselves that we were. Sure, this pup, with his relatives coming from West

Zev had been mild-mannered, kind, and easy to train.

German lines, was going to have more energy and be tougher than Zev. Gentle Zev had loved lying in the grass, sniffing the flowers and clover.

We had nicknamed Zev "Ferdinand," after the peaceful Spanish bull who had no interest in fighting in the ring but wanted to chill in the meadow.

And we didn't plan to upend our lives because of a new puppy. We already had a dog who took a chunk of our time and energy—a beautiful female Irish setter we had adopted from my father several years before. I told David it would be fun, a grand adventure, to adopt a spacey year-old Irish setter and drive across the United States in August with her.

I had lied.

Megan was now four years old, and we no longer fantasized about sending her to a nice farm in the country.

But my feelings about Irish setters hadn't changed much. When I was a child, they filled our small house in Oregon with their joy, their disobedience, and their uncanny ability to bolt around our legs and out the door.

They would disappear into the fog of the Willamette

I grew up with Irish setters. They liked to run.
Often far, far away, with us running after them.

Valley and end up lost, miles away from our little house on the hill. Always at night.

Their other sins were small. They loved to jump on guests and sneak onto our beds and easy chairs.

My father loved their moments of mutiny, loved to stroke their silky heads. They distracted him from a grinding work schedule. Their minor mischief-making was his only vacation.

Even as a child, I loved German shepherds. I loved their intelligence and dignity, their heroic acts in books and movies. I loved the way they looked—like wolves. A dog scientist could have told me that Irish setters were as closely related to wolves as German shepherds—and that the German shepherd was created as a breed in 1899. It didn't matter. I'd had two fine shepherds, Tarn and Zev.

And now, a third.

That night, after I'd finished reading all about singletons and their issues, David and I realized the squashy-faced pup needed a name that suited him better than Coda.

His entry into the world, and his pending entrance into our lives, didn't feel like a thoughtful summary anymore. David, who loves jazz, renamed him "Solo."

Solo is also an Italian musical term. It means "alone."

CHAPTER TWO

· · · · · · · · · ·

THE BRAT KING

Joan nicknamed the singleton pup "HRH." His Royal Highness. She also started calling him Solo, so he would know his name by the time we came for him.

Solo was the king of everything. He had the puppy equivalent of an Ivy League education. Coming from a litter of one has lots of advantages.

Because he was a puppy, he had no idea that we worried about his future as a juvenile delinquent. Joan took him everywhere with her: to hardware stores, to friends' houses, on walks in the woods, to her acupuncture appointments. I followed his adventures via e-mails and photos.

He had everything a puppy could desire, and more.

Everything, that is, except other puppies to play with and learn from. His young mother didn't set a good example. Vita's idea of mothering Solo was to allow him to nurse briefly. Then she'd leap up and race away, like Road Runner running from Wile E. Coyote, leaving him in a cloud of dust.

Luckily, Solo had been born into an extended family, with German shepherd aunts and uncles and cousins—all living in the same household or nearby. So Solo's great-aunt Cora, along with Joan and her husband, Peter, set about the task of raising him.

Cora had fawn-colored fur and a sweet face. She also had a great sense of humor and tolerance for unusual

Cora loved toys, fun, and—of course— Solo.

Photo courtesy of Joan Andreasen-Webb

puppies. She had been one herself. Solo interested and amused her. She taught him to love toys and games.

Sadly, she didn't teach him manners. He got away with everything. In one picture Solo walked across Cora's reclined body, carrying his favorite stuffed duck. His big puppy paws left dents in her plush fur.

At least Solo's head no longer looked squashy and squint-eyed. Now even I could see that his head was going to be gorgeous. A chunk of that little block of beauty contained his olfactory system.

Photo by Sherri Clendenin

Solo, four weeks old, already loved to use his nose.

RIFFING ON SNIFFING

The part of a dog brain
devoted to smelling is
forty times bigger than ours.
    Humans smell and
breathe through the same
space in our noses. A dog has
a fold of tissue just inside
its nose that helps separate
breathing and smelling.

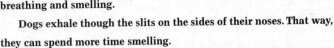

Dogs exhale though the slits on the sides of their noses. That way, they can spend more time smelling.

Dogs can detect some odors, like amyl acetate (a chemical that smells like bananas), at less than two parts per trillion. That's like a drop or two of water in an Olympic-size swimming pool!

Even in the middle of a fast run toward Joan, he would often screech to a halt, nostrils flaring at some wayward scent. "His nose rules," Joan said.

That wasn't welcome news. Megan, our Irish setter, froze at the sight of a bird, cat, or squirrel—every nerve alight and devoted to that one task. She didn't even have to smell them. All she had to do was see them, and she ignored anything else, including us.

I had planned for a dog who would focus only on me— and maybe on David from time to time. I knew it would take a year or so to get Solo up to speed. But the nose thing wasn't going to work. I'd always watched with a touch of scorn as people with flop-jowled bassets and beagles pleaded with their dogs to raise their snorkeling noses off the ground and pay attention to them. I was sure I could train Solo to let sensory organs other than his nose rule.

· · · · · · · · · · · ·

In mid-May, David and I drove the four hundred fifty miles from North Carolina to Ohio to meet and pick up Solo.

He was lying alone on the front lawn in a wire pen when we arrived, clad in plush russet-and-black fur, relaxed, surveying his kingdom.

When Solo met us for the first time, he wasn't impressed.

Photo by David Auerbach

He was only nine weeks old but already past the brief cute phase that shepherd pups have, when their ears are soft and floppy, and their noses don't yet look like shark snouts.

Solo gazed at us briefly when we got out of the car and approached his pen. He sniffed us through the open wire, then ignored us.

Once Joan arrived and let him loose in the backyard, he ran around grabbing at toys and pushing them at various adult shepherds. He was full of himself. He made me slightly nervous.

Joan had arranged a lovely dog-and-people party to launch us back down the road to North Carolina. Solo ran, growled, and leaped during the entire event. He was beyond a brat. He was a bully.

He said farewell to his dignified sire, Quando, by grabbing and holding on to his bright gold scruff. He finally dropped off when Quando looked down his long patrician nose and backed up slightly.

So Solo turned and bit Joan instead.

David and I gathered Solo up, along with a dozen toys (his hedgehog, his duck, and all the offerings that Joan's friends brought to honor HRH), and drove back down the Ohio country road toward North Carolina. In the rear seat, locked in a plastic travel crate for his safety and ours, lay our furry future.

It was a long, hot drive, but Solo didn't mind. When we stopped for breaks, he hopped out of the car, wagging, did his business, and clambered back into the crate like a

Solo's sire, Quando, was perturbed by his son's bullying behavior but was too kind to snarl.

miniature adult shepherd. He loved the car. He didn't bite me. I started feeling less nervous.

"Oh my," said our friend Barb, who arrived that night to witness the homecoming. She had taken care of Megan. Now she watched as Solo leaped on Megan and bit her ears and tail. "He's quite something, isn't he?"

David and I were exhausted. Megan drooled and panted in distress. My arms had puncture marks where Solo had swung back on me, biting me in a frenzy when I tried to come between him and his Irish setter victim.

I was used to puppies nipping me; this felt more like a school of piranhas had fed on my arms.

Solo spent his first night with us whining and growling, slowly chewing through an expensive fabric show crate. He wanted to continue his fun evening. I cried in David's arms. I wanted Zev back. Zev's worst sin had been to take a bar of soap from the shower and place it carefully on the bathroom floor with one faint canine-tooth dent to demonstrate his boredom if we were out of the house.

"I don't like him," I wailed above Solo's whines.

David firmly and kindly said exactly the wrong thing: "We'll just return him."

My sobs increased. I was miserable. Inconsolable.

In the morning I woke up, and even before drinking coffee, I armed myself. I strapped on a belly pack loaded with greasy liver treats. I picked up a plastic-and-metal clicker that would make a metallic *tock* to mark the exact behavior I wanted.

I would ignore his misbehavior. I would reward the good. The little monster. I would shape and mold him with clicks and treats and patience. He would be dog putty. Or at least he'd stop trying to leap on top of Megan. I had abandoned the fantasy of a shepherd sleeping in my study while I wrote.

The clicks and treats helped. But Solo himself changed my mind. David and I both fell hard for him. I fell harder because my emotions always yo-yo further than David's. By midday I was laughing and in love. Solo was a clown, a comic. He was funny, even charming.

He thought David and I were the cat's pajamas, the

bee's knees. He told us all about it. He mewled, growled, barked, howled, yowled, whimpered, and moaned. I'd never heard that kind of vocal variety except on National Geographic specials about the wild dogs of Africa.

On an hourly basis Solo stared at us, made a *roooo* sound to get our attention, and then tried a gymnastic move he thought might please us. He wasn't the king of

The wild dogs of Africa have the most complex and varied language of any canid. Except perhaps Solo.

everything; he was the court jester. He found toys and leaped on them and brought them to us and dropped them and backed up.

He played and played and played. With us. Not with Megan. He occasionally tried to bite her, and she would slink under the dining room table. She was so boring.

He tried to bite us, but he was so tired, he collapsed in our laps and fell asleep, twitching. When he woke, he stared at us. Game on. If he wasn't sleeping, he was watching us, waiting for the Next Big Thing. Thank goodness it was our summer break, and we weren't teaching. Instead we were getting an education.

That second night I didn't sob. Partly because I was too tired, partly because I realized that we had something strange and wonderful on our hands. David was smug but tried to suppress it. We had, he realized, the smartest dog he had ever known.

Smart didn't mean nice. Megan stared at us in dismay, the whites showing at the edges of her large brown eyes. To handicap Solo a bit more, I soaked her long, feathery ears and tail in bitter-apple spray, so that he was less tempted to use them as his personal swing set.

That second night with Solo, Megan used her entire body like a caterpillar's to hunch her foam bed as far as possible from Solo's crate in the bedroom, inch by inch. I. Do. Not. Like. That. Puppy.

Solo didn't care. Megan was just a dog. Dogs weren't his people. Solo had no litter to miss. We had no need to put a clock in the crate to mimic the sound of siblings' beating hearts. He slept through the night. He was at home alone.

CHAPTER THREE

• • • • • • • • • • •

THE LANGUAGE
OF OUCH

In the week after Solo arrived, David and I devoted ourselves to teaching him the universal language of Ouch! Joan taught him, of course, but Solo forgot. He had new hands to bite.

We yelped every time his sharp puppy teeth hit our skin. Solo didn't relate, though he did cock his head when he heard us yip. It hurt. If a toy lay nearby, we'd grab it and offer it in place of our hands. We learned quickly.

The kind and patient adult shepherds he grew up with never bit him. Solo never experienced pain in exchange for what he doled out.

Since we were humans and were supposed to be patient and kind, we didn't bite him back, or hold or slap his muzzle. Training systems like that often make a problem worse.

We weren't the only ones working on Solo's manners. On day four of Solo's arrival, Megan stopped drooling and looking betrayed. She came out from under the table and gave Solo a queenly bow, front legs on the ground, rear in the air. Permission to play.

She taught Solo a few basic rules to alter his brutish behavior. No more standing over her when she was lying down. So rude! No more huge puppy paws placed on her shoulders. No, sir! No teeth on her tail. Ever.

Solo leaped, and Megan moved sideways a fraction. Solo ended up splayed on the floor, surprised. He hadn't touched her gorgeous setter body. She glanced over at us, mouth slightly open to show her small white teeth and tongue. Smiling.

Within a couple of hours, Megan's long silky tail returned to its former high-flying flag position, though Solo's sharp baby teeth had torn gaps in it.

For the first time since Megan came home with us from Oregon three years before, we were in awe of her. Space cadet Megan had disappeared. In her place was a sleek ninja. We watched as she engaged Solo in play, and then cut off their play if he behaved badly. She manipulated the large, emotionally stunted puppy like a pro. We wanted to know what Megan knew.

During that first week we also watched Solo. I had ignored dogs' noses, but I began to understand what Joan

Megan came out from under the table and
started teaching Solo puppy manners.

meant when she used the term "scent drive" in her e-mails.
One morning David went out to work in our garden. I
left the house with Solo five minutes after that, wanting
to avoid accidents inside. He wasn't interested in peeing.
Instead he put his nose a couple of inches above the warm
stones of our courtyard and started moving fast. Then he
was on the grass, skimming the ground, his big pointy
ears almost scraping the dirt.

Solo didn't lift his head until it butted hard against the
legs of a startled David, who was working in the greenhouse. Solo tracked him a hundred feet from the house,
around two bends, on three different surfaces. Solo's

Photo by Cat Warren

Solo followed David's scent.

whole body wiggled in pleasure, and he bit David's jeans in joy until David "ouched" him.

Solo had done his first "live track" — following a person's footsteps and the scent they leave in the air.

To a tracking or trailing dog, the missing person's invisible scent cloud probably *smells* a lot like Pigpen *looks* in *Peanuts*.

I had a new command Solo loved: "Go find David."

I should have added, "Don't bite him when you find him."

• • • • • • • • • • •

We had Solo for only a few weeks when my father and stepmother, Angie, came to visit from Oregon. Dad, his skin increasingly loose across the big bones of his hands, sat blissfully stroking Megan. He looked tired. I tried

GO FIND DAVID!

A dog tracking or trailing a living person uses:

• ground scent from footprints

• freshly crushed vegetation

• a helpful wind that blows human scent toward the dog

• odors from the person's sweat

• odors from the person's skin cells

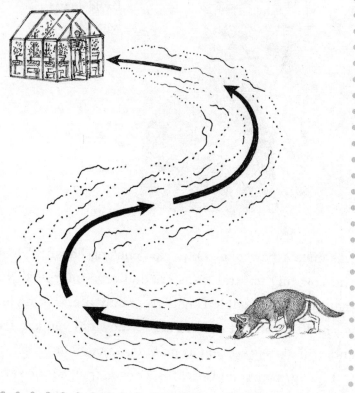

to keep Solo—the opposite of what Dad liked in a dog
personality—well exercised and as far away from the
three of them as possible.

We nourished Dad with David's home-baked bread, black tea at three p.m., a cocktail at five p.m., and long conversations. Dad was glad that I had settled down. I

Solo loved finding David. And I loved David. It was a win-win.

Photo by Cat Warren

was once a newspaper reporter, chasing chemical leaks and covering natural disasters and cruel murders. Now that kind, dependable David was in my life, Dad no longer had to worry. It doesn't matter how old you are. Parents will always see you as no older than eight or ten.

I had grown up in Corvallis, Oregon, judged the safest city in the United States. No earthquakes, no hurricanes, no twisters, no wildfires. Nothing. Dad was secretly pleased that my marriage and job at a university provided as tame a life as when I lived in Oregon, although

North Carolina did get a hurricane every few years.

At one point during Dad and Angie's visit, I must have turned my back. That was when Solo leaped. Blood welled on the back of Dad's hand. He dismissed it with a shrug. Solo was just a puppy. His Irish setters, with their soft mouths and personalities, had never drawn blood.

I put Solo in his crate with a goat knucklebone to gnaw on.

Dad and Angie's weeklong visit ended without further injury, except for Solo attacking and tearing Angie's beautiful chenille bathrobe. Dad and I walked one final time around the yard before they left to fly back across

Photo courtesy of Betty Young

Dad, a biologist in Oregon, loved the plants and birdlife of North Carolina, where I now lived.

the country. The two of us looked at the newly planted blueberry bushes, with names such as rabbiteye and highbush. We admired the male cardinals that dropped like red explosions from the willow oaks to the ground, with their distinct cries of *Chew! Chew! Chew!*

Dad and I talked about how fine the future looked for both of us. But his undiagnosed cancer had probably started spreading through his body that June.

· · · · · · · · · · · ·

Simple commands such as "Sit," "Heel," or "Settle" didn't interest Solo. He obeyed, but always with a twist. His crazy energy ruled. It wasn't enough to go into the mud-room, lie down, and wait for dinner. He had to launch, flip in midair like a skateboarder, and then crouch like a gargoyle, pleased with himself.

He experimented. If he braked hard a few feet before the door, he could slide and do a half somersault. He had a great sense of humor. His great-aunt Cora helped him develop that.

Solo adored David and me more each day. He thought Megan was fun.

But he was completely unpredictable with other dogs and puppies. Mostly he thought they were hostile aliens. Especially German shepherds or other breeds with pointy ears, though he barely tolerated floppy-eared dogs.

When he smelled an unfamiliar dog, he growled, and his fur bristled all down his spine. Visits to the vet ended badly. One vet put in her notes that Solo was on his way to being dangerous. Solo was ten weeks old. I quit her. Another vet said he was growling because he hurt somewhere. She recommended expensive and silly alternative treatments. He wasn't in pain. He *was* a pain. I quit her, too.

Puppy classes were worse. He walked into training centers barking and growling, hackles raised, eyes rolling. The same owners who used to smile when they saw sweet Zev arrive for obedience training snatched up their small shelties and miniature schnauzers at the sight of Solo.

Trainers with decades of experience and obedience trophies on their shelves strategized with me. Perhaps Solo needed a new kind of halter, maybe a Gentle Leader, to guide his wayward muzzle in a direction away from biting?

One trainer I had trained with for years with Zev suggested I needed to discipline Solo severely for his bad behavior. That never works. I quit her.

I was getting good at quitting.

I'd never had a dog-aggressive dog. Solo confirmed what many people thought they already knew: German shepherds were dangerous. I threw myself into trying to fix Solo. I ordered expensive obedience videos. I ordered books on canine aggression.

I was part of Solo's problem. Once I realized he didn't like other dogs, I tensed every time I saw one coming

Photo by David Auerbach

Solo thought other dogs — even sweet puppies
with floppy ears — were hostile aliens.

toward us. My fear about what might happen went from
my trembling hand down his leash and into his blocky
head. My tension confirmed what Solo already knew.
Dogs meant trouble.

We made a terrible team.

My relationships with other dog owners began to suffer.
On a "down-stay" in an obedience class, Solo roared and
leaped on a shorthaired pointer who had bounced over
to greet him. The teacher, who had cheerful Labradors,
looked at me with dismay and shrugged. He was right. It
wasn't entirely Solo's fault.

I snarled under my breath, "Keep your dog on a leash and under control!"

I was at the end of my own leash. I was getting people-aggressive.

I left class early.

I cried again that night in David's arms—angry at Solo, at the stupid pointer owner. At myself.

It was worse than that first night when David suggested sending Solo back. Now I wasn't simply invested in the idea of this German shepherd puppy. I loved him, though I hated his behavior.

He was now mine—my large puppy and my responsibility. He lay quietly in the backseat on the long drives home from puppy obedience classes we were forced to leave early, or that we dropped out of entirely.

I switched training systems. I avoided places where I knew other dogs might be. I stopped taking him for walks in our neighborhood because it was filled with dog owners who expected us to do meet and greets on the street.

I was failing him. I did what I always do: I e-mailed Joan. None of Joan's many shepherds had acted like Solo around other dogs when they were young.

When Solo was born, Joan confessed, she had worried. She knew what we might be facing with a singleton puppy. She called around Ohio, trying to find a litter about the age of HRH that she could place him with, to give him the social life he needed. But no one nearby had a litter close to his age.

"Quite honestly," Joan wrote me, "I am now convinced from years of training, and now Solo, that the majority of puppies missing a complete litter experience just don't learn how to handle the nuances of a variety of dog interaction. They don't learn the give-and-take."

After watching Solo growl and leap, people started asking me: "You named him after Han Solo, right?"

No. I saw *Star Wars* once, and didn't like the character, even though I loved Harrison Ford, who played him.

Yet Solo and Han Solo had a lot in common. They were both charismatic, talented, reckless misfits.

They were loners.

CHAPTER FOUR

. . . .

HOW TO TRAIN YOUR TASMANIAN DEVIL

Two months after Solo barreled into our lives, I found myself in Nancy Hook's backyard in rural North Carolina, perched on the edge of a camping chair. Nancy, an experienced dog trainer, slumped back in her own canvas chair, her hand wrapped around a Gatorade.

I contacted Nancy because I was desperate, and I remembered her sense of humor and practicality from some years before when I'd trained with her. Sure, she said, come on out and let's talk. Bring the dog.

She seemed to be in a good mood, except for the warnings she gave the dogs who were barking and occasionally snarling at one another in her "boot camp" training kennels next to the yard: "Don't make me come over there."

They stopped. It was mid-July and too hot to fight, in any case.

Bronze Japanese beetles buzzed past, intent on their mission to strip the leaves off nearby fruit trees. Tent caterpillars had made themselves a home in the huge pecan tree we sat under.

I first met Nancy when I'd taken Zev to her parking-lot obedience classes. She'd been welcoming and kind to both of us back then, though not particularly interested in Zev. He was so mild-mannered, he disappeared in a dog crowd.

I hadn't seen Nancy much since, but I started to remember her as I pulled into the drive and read the black bumper sticker on her pickup: GUT DEER?

Her hair was still copper red, her dark eyes still surrounded by smile wrinkles. She wore camouflage pants.

She was relaxed. I wasn't. Solo, now four months old, was wild-eyed and bad-mannered. From time to time he made a break toward the kennels. He was a mixture of snarling Tasmanian devil and awkward colt.

He bounced off the cyclone fence. I bounced off my chair, wrestling dog treats out of my belly pack, trying to distract him. "Solo? Solo? Watch me! Gooood dog!" I poured liver treats into his open mouth.

"Stop chattering at him," Nancy said. "And stop giving him so many treats. You're turning him into a wuss."

Tasmanian devil, Chen Wu (CC)/Colt, Pixabay

Tasmanian devil + clumsy colt = four-month-old Solo.

My hand froze on its way to the fanny pack.

"He's just a jackass," she said. "What do you want to do with him?"

That simple question helped stabilize my weird dog world. Nancy didn't think that Solo needed a counselor, or that I had to create a calm and perfect shepherd. And Solo wasn't dog putty. He was just a dog. He had strengths and weaknesses, like each of us.

Nancy meant exactly what she said: What would you like this dog to do?

I had no idea. I wanted him to be so busy that he didn't have time to do what he was doing in front of Nancy. I thought a job might be a good thing for him. Not a pretend job. And he wasn't suited for some real dog jobs. He probably wouldn't be a good therapy dog, visiting with patients in nursing homes. His rhino ways already sent me tumbling.

He didn't know it hurt when he barreled into people.

Nancy didn't let me daydream for long. "Stop thinking so much," she said. "That's part of your problem."

She ordered me to leave Solo alone. I pulled my hands away from the greasy treat bag and put them at my sides. I turned my gaze away from Solo's evilness.

After a couple of minutes, he came over and flopped down in the shade. Being bad isn't as interesting if no one is watching.

Nancy and I talked. Nancy taught dogs pretty much everything: Don't pee on the carpet. Don't bite people. Don't bite other dogs really hard unless they deserve it. She also taught more fascinating tasks, like canine search and rescue—helping find lost people using dogs' noses.

I realized that it wasn't realistic to train Solo with a local search-and-rescue team. I was a teacher and couldn't leave students waiting in a university classroom for me while I ran off with Solo to search for a lost three-year-old who was probably playing at the next-door neighbor's.

I doubted that I could run for miles after a dog tracking a lost hunter in thick underbrush. I would end up wheezing, eyeglasses fogged or smashed. I'd need someone to rescue me.

Besides, I didn't want to wear a search uniform. Lots of people love them, and I understand that. I wasn't one of those people. Then there was the idea of a team. I could cooperate, but I was never one to relate to the cheery phrase "Remember, there is no *I* in 'team.'"

The setup wasn't great for Solo, either. Search teams almost always require their dogs to be dog-friendly. I imagined how quickly tempers would flare and fur would fly. Solo and I would slink off, once again.

There was one way around the scheduling problems, my team-player problems, and Solo's psycho-puppy problems. Nancy was pleased with herself. "Why don't you train him as a cadaver dog?"

I didn't know exactly what Nancy meant, but I could guess. "Dead dog." I'm good at putting words together.

Nancy explained what a cadaver dog did. I was intrigued. When someone is missing, it's important to find them, even when you know they are dead. Recovering someone's body is an important stage for law enforcement and for family and friends. That is where a cadaver dog can be invaluable.

After people die and start to decompose, just as animals do, they start to smell different. A cadaver dog is trained to find that particular smell. Human scent is unique, both while we are alive and after we die. That's a good thing, as a well-trained cadaver dog can use his nose to help find someone who is missing and dead.

Cadaver dogs and their handlers work mostly by themselves, in a kind of grid pattern, with the dogs usually off lead so that they can range freely to catch a hint of scent if it's out there. Best of all, they don't work closely alongside other dogs and handlers. I liked that idea a lot. I knew Solo liked to use his nose, but not when other dogs were around.

And it was an intriguing way to tire him out. Nancy told me that her German shepherd Indy had been both a search-and-rescue dog and a cadaver dog. Because of his impossible energy, Indy had changed owners twice before Nancy found him. Once he had an outlet for that drive, he stayed with Nancy.

I wasn't grossed out by the whole idea. The thought of finding a human body didn't frighten me although I hadn't done it yet. But everyone dies. It's the circle of life and life on this planet.

Nancy made cadaver-dog work sound as if it were an ideal solution for Solo's problems and my work schedule. Although finding dead bodies is demanding, you can

Photo courtesy of Nancy Hook

Nancy's dog Indy searched for both the living and the dead.

often work with the police to schedule searches. While it's important, it's not as immediately urgent as trying to find someone alive. The dead can wait.

A cadaver dog's job is both simple and complex: to go to where the scent is the strongest and tell the handler it's there. It's work that needs to be done, even if someone has been missing for years.

Besides, Nancy told me, her laugh lines in full evidence, "It's a ton of fun. You'll love it!"

It sounds funny, but I knew exactly what she meant. It was fascinating, honest work, both for me and for the dog. Solo's nose and energy might combine nicely with my love of the woods, science, and nature. And I love to read mysteries.

At the end of our session, Nancy sent me and Solo off down her rural road. I was sweaty, I reeked of liver treats, and I was filled with an odd elation about people who go missing for a long, long time.

Solo slept soundly in the backseat, though his huge paws continued to twitch.

Nancy, who knew some of my bad habits, told me not to read too much about scent-detection dogs. I'd confuse myself and the dog.

Of course, I disobeyed her. As soon as I got home, I got onto the computer to learn about how to train a dog to find someone, living or dead. I also delved into the ancient relationship between death and dogs. I knew Nancy wouldn't mind my learning about that.

• • • • • • • • • • • •

In 2011 archaeologists in the Czech Republic found three skulls of what appeared to be domesticated dogs. The animals had shorter muzzles and broader heads than their wolf cousins. One of the skulls, nearly thirty-two thousand years old, had a bone fragment, probably a mammoth's, resting in its jaws.

Dog skull discovered in the Czech Republic, with a bone sticking out between its front teeth.

The skull, holding a bone like it was a stick, seemed so staged that the archaeologists had to wonder: Had someone placed that bone in the dog's jaws as part of an ancient ceremony to coax the dog to stay with its human into the afterlife?

As archaeologists, anthropologists, and scientists study ancient sites and the bones and DNA of early dogs, they learn more each year about how humans and dogs evolved together.

Our relationship with dogs is a long one. And every

time one mystery is solved, every time scientists think they know the answer, another dog-and-human mystery emerges.

That's because the relationship between dogs and humans is complicated. This coevolution stretches for tens of thousands of years and clear across the world.

We changed dogs and dogs changed us.

One of the most complicated parts of this relationship is the one that dogs have with human death. For thousands of years, in numerous religions and cultures, people have depended on canines to help guide the dead—to help us get from here to there, wherever or whatever "there" means.

Overall, the world seems less frightening with a dog at your side. That is especially true when one faces death. In numerous religions, from Hinduism in India to the ancient Mayan and Aztec religions in Mesoamerica, the dead depend on canines to guide them to the next world.

Dogs seem made for this task. They howl at the moon. They hear and smell things we can't. They warn us that someone—or something—is coming, long before our dull human senses tell us.

But older cultures knew that many canids, such as wolves, coyotes, jackals, and dogs, were scavengers. That meant they weren't afraid to approach the dead—and even eat them if they needed the calories.

Today in the West, the thought horrifies us. Back then, though, many cultures came to an interesting conclusion: dogs and their close relatives were so powerful that they didn't fear the demons of death. Canids didn't mind getting close to demon-filled bodies. And that was a good thing.

So in ancient Egypt a large-eared jackal-dog became a god. Anubis protected the deceased in their tombs.

Photo by Tookapic

Artwork and statues showing Anubis, the Egyptian god of the dead, protecting tombs and graves are dated as early as 3100 BC. Now some genetic scientists think Anubis might have been a golden wolf.

In ancient Persia, the area we now call Iran, a religious people called Zoroastrians especially loved dogs. They used them to herd their sheep and goats, and to hunt game. They kept dogs as beloved house pets.

But the thing that interested me most? They used dogs for funerals, to scare away Nasu, the death demon. The funeral service in Zoroastrianism included a part called *sagdid*, which means "seen by the dog." According to the ancient texts, it took a special kind of dog for this work.

The ideal sagdid dog needed to be at least four months old and male, "brownish-golden," with "four eyes" — which probably referred to the different-colored spots of fur that some dogs have over their eyes.

If Solo lived in Persia thousands of years ago, with his twitchy black spots of fur over his eyes, he might have enjoyed being a sagdid dog. The dog could also be white or yellow with tawny ears. They may have looked like the Canaan dog of Israel, a now-rare ancient herding and guard breed.

Photo by Cindy Obitz

Lachan, who lives in France with his owner, Cindy Obitz, is one of only a few thousand Canaan dogs in the world today.

The dogs chosen for sagdid got paid for their work. Zoroastrians knew their dog training, just like Nancy. They put three pieces of bread on the deceased person's body. The dog's job was pretty simple: to approach the body and stare at it. Of course, the dog was probably staring at the bread.

That didn't matter. The stare sufficed to drive the demon Nasu away.

● ● ● ● ● ● ● ● ● ● ●

It wasn't all that different from how Nancy taught me to train Solo. From the beginning he was happy to approach the scent of human death. All it meant to him was that he was going to get a reward. I used liver treats rather than bread. I doubted Solo would work as hard for a measly bit of bread.

My early research on dogs and death, and on cadaver dogs, didn't change my mind about whether I could do this work. I knew there was a difference between reading about it and having Solo and me actually find a body. But the idea of finding cadavers using dogs didn't scare me. It fascinated me.

And I realized that Solo, though he was still a puppy, was going to be a large dog. If I went out into the woods on a search, I wouldn't be alone. Solo would be at my side. Or in front of me.

Perhaps a touch of Tasmanian devil in him wasn't such a bad thing.

OUR OLDEST BEST FRIEND?

Middle East cliffside art shows curly-tailed dogs that look like Canaan dogs hunting alongside people perhaps eight thousand years ago. Later, Canaan dogs guarded ancient Israelite camps and helped herd flocks of sheep. When the Romans destroyed Jerusalem in AD 70, the intelligent and wily dogs escaped into the desert—and survived.

In the mid-1930s, Austrian immigrant Rudolphina Menzel raised and trained these now-wild dogs for the Jewish paramilitary in the Middle East. It took six months to capture her first Canaan dog, named Dugma, but within weeks, she could take him into town and on buses.

CHAPTER FIVE

· · · · · · · · · ·

THE WHOLE TOOTH

A few weeks after Nancy Hook and I discussed Solo's future, we were back in her training yard. Solo stood, brow wrinkled, staring at five white plastic buckets Nancy had lined up with military precision.

One of them contained a glass jar with a tooth in it. For Solo's first exposure to cadaver scent, Nancy used one of her soon-to-be-ex-husband's wisdom teeth, packed with a bit of bloody gauze.

Solo, nearly five months old, was fifty-five pounds of raw bone and sinew—and attitude. Few young German shepherds are handsome. Solo wasn't. Despite my ongoing nightmares, he didn't land far outside the shepherd mainstream in looks or behavior.

Nancy explained what Solo's job was: to duck his head inside each bucket, sniff, and figure out which one held the tooth and gauze. She even put empty jars inside the other buckets so we'd know that we weren't accidentally training Solo to find jars out in the woods.

Buckets are one of many methods to start a cadaver dog, or any scent-detection dog. Solo needed to both recognize the scent of human remains and tell me he had found it.

All I needed to bring to the party was perfect timing.

On the first run past the buckets, Solo ducked his

BOXES OR BUCKETS OR BLOCKS? WHAT WOULD YOU USE?

- • Wooden boxes
- • Cardboard boxes
- • Concrete blocks
- • Plastic pipes
- • Metal cans
- • Plastic buckets

Everyone has a favorite training system for "foundation work." What's important is that the containers all look alike and only one of the containers has the material you want the dog to find.

Eleven-year-old Haylee Carney works with her new cadaver dog, Jayda, on a series of PVC pipes in a circle, and rewards her for finding the target scent.

Photo by Cat Warren

head into the fourth bucket, which held the still-bloody tooth, looked at me, then ducked his head back in.

Something in that bucket smelled different from the first three buckets.

Nancy hissed at me. I fumbled to give him a liver treat. He needed to associate that smell with a reward. He needed to get that reward instantly. Solo helped himself to the tip of my finger along with the treat. He still didn't get the "biting equals hurt" equation.

He loved the game: Sniff. Bite fingers. Get treat.

Nancy switched the position of the buckets, so the tooth was in the third bucket. Solo charged from one to the next, jerking me along, tying us up together in his leather lead, pulling his head out of the bucket with the tooth, staring at me, griping loudly if I didn't reward him immediately. His yowls moved up and down the scales, from delight to frustration.

Nancy's chestnut eyes narrowed as she watched us perform the funky chicken dance. Solo led. I heard my heart forcing blood through my head.

The directions were simple. I was to move ahead of Solo, using a loose lead, past each bucket, not hesitating, not rushing. With a gracious hand gesture, I was to present the bucket to him. Check here (dog's head dips into the bucket), check here (dog's head dips into the next bucket), check here (dog's head dips and stays close to the tooth). Good dog! Treat! That constant positive reinforcement would help Solo realize that recognizing and reacting to that smell would bring treats or a toy his way.

Nancy let me keep the treats in my handy belly pack this time. I wasn't funneling them into his mouth to distract him. I was using them to teach a new skill.

But the treats were turning out to be one more thing to manage in addition to the leash, the dog, the buckets— and my dignity, which I kept losing.

Solo surged from one bucket to the next, skipping one that didn't seem interesting, doubling back to make sure, yanking me hard, then yowling when he got a whiff of scent and changed his mind about which bucket to pick.

He was energetic and out of control. Nancy loved it. She chuckled and crooned, "Good boy, good boy." She hissed at me, "Reward him, reward him!"

I was near tears. I didn't fully understand that Solo was in what working-dog trainers call "drive" mode. That's when a dog is both revved up and focused, so excited about a job that he takes off like a race car.

I thought Solo was in "bad dog" mode.

Zev had walked quietly and steadily at my side in a perfect heel. He got depressed if I scowled at him. Even Megan, though she didn't care if I approved of what she did, was obedience-trained and gentle.

Solo was brutally adjusting my canine worldview. According to Nancy, I had my first "working dog." Sweet, docile dogs were boring, and Nancy wanted nothing to do with them. Solo was making me miserable and doing exactly what Nancy wanted.

I could feel her looking at me, eyebrows raised, as I fumbled for treats. I was trying my best, but I couldn't coordinate my arms and legs.

"That's it," Nancy said when she heard Solo yodeling at me for about the third time because he wasn't getting rewarded fast enough. "There's his alert!"

If I hadn't been so frustrated, I would have marked this as a special moment. An alert, or what some dog trainers call a "final indication," is supposed to be something that comes naturally to the dog. It's the dog's way of signaling clearly to the handler, "I've got it!"

Most law enforcement dogs trained to find illegal drugs sit with a focused stare at the spot where the drug smell is strongest. For instance, a dog will sit close to the trunk of a car and stare at the crack of the trunk, because that's where the scent is drifting out, even if the illegal drugs are hidden deep in the trunk.

A few narcotics dogs might still dig or scratch at the trunk, though that "aggressive alert" is disappearing. Bomb dogs are trained to never scratch or dig, for obvious reasons.

Nancy explained that Solo's impatient whine combined with a sit might become his trained alert to tell me he had not only found the material we were looking for, but he was also committing himself to that one spot.

More important, I could tell law enforcement before a search started, "This is what Solo will do if he detects the odor of human remains. He'll sit and scream at me."

A real search wasn't in our immediate future. If it ever came. Finding a tooth in a bucket and telling me was a baby step along the long road to mastery.

I was a doofus that day. I was thinking about everything other than Solo's nose—his big feet, my clumsy feet, and Nancy judging me.

It wasn't until much later that I had time to ponder. How did Solo figure out so quickly which bucket held the tooth?

•   •   •   •   •   •   •   •   •   •   •

Even before I started training Solo, I heard dogs had good noses. I'd seen Solo's in action. I wasn't blind. Solo's nose had to be better than mine. David could use a pair of scissors on a package of vacuum-sealed steak in the kitchen, and the silent exhalation of bloody air would wake Solo and bring him running from across the room. I couldn't smell that meat until my nose was a couple of inches away, or it had seared in the frying pan a few minutes.

Before, when I watched the news on the television, read the newspaper, or heard the occasional story about dogs tracking someone for miles, I didn't pay a lot of attention when everyone said that dogs' sense of smell was miraculous.

Now that I was concentrating on it, I became suspicious.

Sure, Solo has a bigger nose than I do. But size isn't everything. What was the truth about Solo and the tooth?

The truth is, scientists are still learning. Even humans' sense of smell isn't entirely understood.

In the meantime, we now take for granted that the dog's nose is the ideal tool for finding things that we humans can't. Why? Because it seems to work.

I was training Solo to recognize the smell of a tooth and, down the road, to recognize the scent of a huge range of human remains, from old bone or blood to someone who was recently murdered.

But the list of things that dogs can be trained to find? Almost endless—from anteaters to zebra mussels.

Well-trained scent dogs are great at finding people, too. Lost people, violent people, missing people.

Using hunting dogs to find wildlife dates back many thousands of years. Human tracking and avalanche-rescue work originated centuries ago.

But using dogs to find bombs, drugs, and the dead? That's much more recent.

I dove into the research about dogs and their olfactory abilities. I immediately became confused and dizzy. No one could agree. The dog's nose was ten times or a hundred times or a thousand times or tens of thousands of times better than the human nose.

PEANUTS, PYTHONS, AND PEOPLE

The list of what a well-trained scent-detection dog can find grows longer every day!

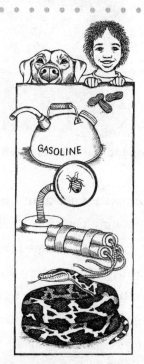

• Accelerant used by an arsonist

• Bedbugs hanging out in a hotel

• Pythons preying in the Everglades

• TNT that triggers explosions

• Peanuts that trigger allergies

• And best of all? People!

Photo by Cat Warren

A bloodhound follows a trail laid two hours earlier by a helper.

Animal Planet didn't think thousands of times better was enough. On "Top 10 Animal Skills" *Creature Countdowns*, they proclaimed that the bloodhound's nose is "up to a million times more sensitive than that of humans."

I'm not a detective, but that number seemed kind of exaggerated. A million? Why not a billion? Or a trillion?

Dog scientists started off by counting the number of scent-receptor cells inside a nose. The bigger the number, the better the nose, most dog experts said.

At first I believed them. I found Solo's breed on a scent-receptor spreadsheet. His German shepherd's nose ranked below a bloodhound's but well above most other breeds'.

Given the variation, I started to wonder: Exactly how much better is a dog nose than a human nose? What about a bear nose? Was one dog breed's nose really better than another's? Might Solo be better than a wine steward at sniffing out the difference between a burgundy and a Bordeaux? Was his nose really the same as a beagle's?

I had no answers, but Solo was starting to teach me. I knew he used his nose. I knew he used it to find meat in the kitchen and David in the greenhouse.

And thanks to Nancy, I now knew that he could find things that carried only a whiff of scent.

All it took was a tooth.

SPECIES	NUMBER OF SCENT RECEPTORS
HUMAN	5 MILLION
DACHSHUND	125 MILLION
FOX TERRIER	147 MILLION
BEAGLE	225 MILLION
GERMAN SHEPHERD	225 MILLION
BLOODHOUND	300 MILLION

Figures by Stanley Coren

CHAPTER SIX

. . . .

THE MAGICIAN

The good and the bad about learning new things is that you want to learn more. Immediately. So before I could say, "Shazam!" I was on a plane to Seattle to meet a magician.

Canadian Kevin George is a master dog trainer. He's trained an elephant. And a bear. He's been a cop and a rodeo clown. He's also an amateur magician.

Before all that, Kevin was a kid who loved magic tricks. He learned how to make his fingers furl and then unfurl like birds set free, how to pluck a coin from behind a friend's ear, and how to manipulate a deck of playing cards.

If you love magic as a kid, if you're lucky, you can

Kevin George trained an elephant, a bear, and lots of dogs.
Most of all, he trains people. They are a lot more work.

keep doing it when you grow up. Kevin's work is serious. He trains dogs to bite bad guys, to search for drugs, to track lost children and criminals, to find people alive. Sadly, sometimes to find them dead. But he always keeps his sense of humor—and his love of a clever trick.

The shell game is one of the oldest tricks in the world. Today it goes by many names: three-cup shuffle or three-card monte are the most common. Illustrations of people playing the shell game date back to ancient Greece, when players used seashells with a dried pea hidden under one of them. People watching the game were rarely successful at guessing where the pea was because the player was so good at misdirecting or using sleight of hand to mislead the person watching.

Today people use playing cards or a few cups and a ball. The queen of hearts is never where the victim, or mark, thinks she is. The ball is never under the cup the mark points at.

But the saying "A fool and his money are soon parted" is always true.

Three-cup shuffle sounds more like a human game than a dog game. But in 1978, Kevin had a German shepherd police K9 who didn't want to search properly. The work was one big yawn.

That's bad. If there's a dangerous and violent person hidden in a warehouse, and the dog isn't interested in covering the whole area to find that person and tell the handler he's there, it can end with injuries or death for the police or the dog.

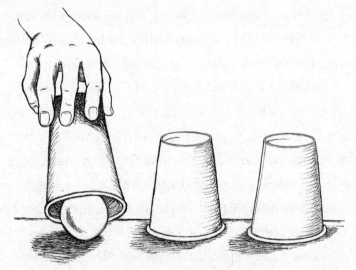

The player shows where the ball is
before quickly shuffling the cups.

Kevin wondered: Could he use magic to motivate his dog? He wanted the dog to search with enthusiasm, to quarter back and forth properly, to cover the search area. To be engaged in his work. To be willing to stick his head into confined spaces, like a closet, if needed. To not get distracted.

It was a tall order, but Kevin started thinking how a dog version of three-cup shuffle might work. Kevin practices and teaches the purest kind of dog magic: the art of misdirection and the craft of sleight of hand. A trainer's job isn't to train the dog but to train the dog handler. Dog training is easy. People training is harder. So Kevin created the box game. He uses cardboard boxes instead of cups, and a dog's favorite toy instead of a small ball.

The box game helps handlers think inside the box. Because I hadn't brought Solo with me, Kevin chose me to be his magician's assistant for his show.

It was hot that fall day in Seattle. The dogs were panting. I was sweating. Kevin—a humorous, white-haired magician—sat in the minimal shade, and I followed his orders. That was fine. I suspected Kevin didn't plan to saw me in half or throw knives at me.

All that was needed for Kevin's magic show were some search-and-rescue dogs and cadaver dogs, their human handlers, and six cardboard boxes in a parallel line on a lawn. I looked inside each of them. No doves. No teeth. Nada.

"Any fool can take a great dog and make it greater."
Kevin George trains dogs to eat only on command.

As a magician's assistant, I probably shouldn't betray the magician's secret, but Kevin gave me permission. My job was to stand there, expressionless, holding each dog in turn on a fairly short leash. It sounds easy, but it was hard for me to keep my mouth shut and not pet the dog.

Every single dog at the show—from the blind English spaniel, to the squat guy who looked like a mix between a pug and a beagle, to the pretty little Chesapeake Bay retriever named Truffle—became a victim in Kevin George's game of six-box shuffle.

First Kevin directed the handlers to make fools of themselves.

"If you can't act like a crazy person, you will not be a good dog handler. Don't be scared to do things that make you interesting to the dog."

I held the first dog, and the handler started acting goofy. She shook her dog's favorite stuffed rabbit in front of his nose. She then ran away, screaming, shaking the rabbit as if breaking its little neck. She ran to a cardboard box and made a big deal of holding the toy right over it.

The dog, like a crowd member watching a game of three-cup shuffle, stared intently. He couldn't help it. Most dogs love to hunt. The toy disappeared into the cardboard box, like a rabbit going down its hole. The handler ran back to her dog, who was pulling like crazy on my arm. I tried not to wince. I handed the leash over, and the handler unclipped the dog. The dog dashed to the box, with the handler close behind. Bam. Toy retrieved. Big happy, joy, joy.

We did the same thing a second time. The dog knew he couldn't lose. He watched. He knew which box the rabbit was in. He had eyes. How simple. Stupid handler. Stupid assistant.

The third time, the game changed. The handler ran to box one and only pretended to put the toy in the box.

Then she moved to box two and—blocking the dog's view—put the toy into the second box. She returned to the first box and made a fuss, pretending the rabbit was in box one. She shook that box like the rabbit was trying to escape.

Kevin again noted how important it was to be melodramatic.

Set loose, the dog ran to box one. Nothing. The box had the owner's scent, the toy's scent, even the dog's scent. But no toy.

The dog looked puzzled. Then betrayed. The dog used his paw and flipped the box over. Nothing. He looked at his handler, who appeared as indifferent as I did. No help coming from us. The dog glanced over and saw another box a few feet away. Perhaps he got a little whiff of his toy, since the wind was coming in the right direction.

He ran to the second box. Whoa! Look! My rabbit!

Everyone cheered. The dog pranced and shook his rabbit hard. He was full of himself. Like Solo. Like someone now sure he could beat the dealer in three-cup shuffle.

"When people get interested, they can get hooked hard-core. They don't like not being successful," Kevin pointed out. They will put more and more money down on a game or a bet.

The dog didn't have money. Instead he offered more intensity and interest in the game. I was starting to understand the word "drive."

The dog was hooked, but so were we. We were fascinated and a little scornful. It had been so easy to trick the dog. Stupid dog.

Kevin crossed his hands over his stomach and smiled. His favorite part of the magic trick was next.

A dog has a huge advantage over a human. Dogs have eyes and ears, sure. But for search-and-rescue dogs, or other detection dogs, there's another sensory organ that's crucial—especially when it's used to overrule the other senses.

OUR SHREWD ANCESTORS

One of the earliest mammal cousins of dogs—and us!—was a shrew-like critter with a skull smaller than a paper clip.

It scurried around nearly two hundred million years ago, probably at night to sniff for smelly grubs and insects. That way, dinosaurs roaming during the day didn't squash it by accident.

Its fur was important, its twitchy ears important, its vision important.

Though its fur and good hearing helped this creature survive, its sense of smell was its most important power. That's what helped make the brain of the tiny *Hadrocodium wui* so large.

And that's what put mammals like us a nose ahead.

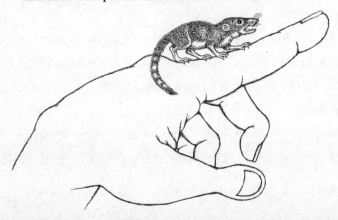

The dog realized that he couldn't trust his own eyes or ears, or his handler. So he stopped relying on them. He stopped believing what he saw. He stopped looking at his handler for help.

Using his olfactory system, the dog found his toy rabbit. Every time. He searched every box, using that system.

Soon all the dogs were methodically and rapidly searching up to eight boxes that were now upside down and scattered clear across the lawn. They ignored their handlers, flipped the boxes over with their noses, gave quick sniffs, and then moved on until they found their toys.

They were no longer marks of the box-shuffle trick. They were detection dogs.

Using box magic, Kevin had trained the handlers to convince their dogs to commit more and more interest to the hunt. All those years before, he turned his bored patrol K9 into an eager search dog. Now he passed that gift on.

"The dog itself always has a high degree of interest," he said. "They're very aware of what's going on around them. The simplest thing will draw them in if it's intriguing enough."

As more and more boxes were added, "It should look like fanning cards." As Kevin talked, his hand was in a fist. Then he spread his fingers open, one by one, in a fluid movement.

Weirdly enough, the dogs' work started looking like that fist unfurling. The dogs sniffed and flipped, sniffed and flipped. They almost flowed among the boxes, sorting scent like pros: no, no, no, no, YES!

Nearly twenty dogs worked that day—all shapes, sizes, and personalities. They were hooked. They all wanted the same thing. The big, dog-aggressive chocolate Labrador, who had been getting up in the muzzles of other dogs, realized better stuff could be found in the boxes. Dogs? What dogs? Where's my toy?

I thought about Solo and what he might do. I missed him. He was 2,851 miles away, in Durham. I knew he'd love this box game. I'd just need a magician's assistant willing to hang on to the leash of an obnoxious German shepherd.

CHAPTER SEVEN

• • • • • • • • • • •

A FISH PIPE AND A HANDBOOK

One day when we arrived at Nancy's training yard, she had a present waiting for us. I was expecting white buckets. Instead she pulled the handmade gift out of her canvas pants pocket and gave it to me. I took it gingerly. It was a piece of white plastic plumber's pipe, about two inches in diameter and nine inches long, drilled full of small holes, its end caps glued shut.

What was most important was inside—a bit of cloth that had rested underneath a body for some time. Its odor seeped gently through the holes. I sniffed cautiously. An old, independent woman, increasingly vague with dementia, had wandered away from her cabin in the Appalachian Mountains. They found her body a couple of weeks later.

I thought I knew the smell of human decay. But this smell wasn't the cloying sweetness I remembered. Instead it was light and dry. More like mold on an orange. That twist of cloth from underneath her body was enough to train Solo for the moment. I hoped she hadn't suffered.

We called the pipe "Fish." Nancy liked the name because it didn't sound like any other command. It had a nice, soft hissing sound to it. The fish pipe would teach Solo that the odor of the deceased was what he should hunt for, wherever it was. Mostly it wouldn't be sitting in a white bucket, even though the buckets would still come in handy for training.

Nancy took the pipe back from me and then showed it to Solo. "Good Fish," she said in a conversational tone.

He sniffed. Sure. Whatever. Interesting, but not as distracting as Nancy's German shepherd Whiskey, snarling behind the fence.

Then Nancy started to gambol about like the cartoon character Goofy, nimble and silly. As Kevin George said, if you can't act like a crazy person, you can't be a good dog trainer. Nancy whipped the pipe around in big circles, away from Solo. She made the fish pipe the equivalent of a live rabbit. Now it was more exciting than Whiskey.

Solo chased it. Nancy teased him more, encouraged him to grab it, then pulled it away at the last minute. He followed her, grabbed it, and tugged hard. Mine at last!

He pranced around with the fish pipe in his mouth. He looked sillier than Nancy.

Solo loved the fish pipe. I loved it too. It helped him understand that from now on he should find that scent, wherever it was. The scent was now a search. It was rarely going to be right in front of him in a white bucket.

The fish pipe got to play many roles. At first I tossed it out into the yard so that Solo could retrieve it and play with it. Next, Fish was hidden in an easy spot in the yard or woods. "Go find your Fish!"

The next step was harder. I showed Fish to Solo and pretended to throw it. Then I tucked it in my back pocket.

Fish was now a signal to start searching. I held out my

Solo thought the present Nancy gave us was a ton of fun.
But a serious purpose lay behind it.

empty hands. "Where's Fish?" Out in the yard, I'd already planted a glass jar with training material in it. That was what he needed to find. The first few times, he stared at me hard. I know where Fish is. It's in your back pocket. I could get it, you know.

Then he entered into the game, bounding away from me.

Two months after Nancy started Solo and me on our

Solo suddenly smelled hidden cadaver-training material, and it stopped him mid-run.

clumsy bucket dance, his brain, his nose, and his body started to work as a unit.

I e-mailed Joan: "He was literally running right past the hidden mason jar with the cheesecloth lid. Scent was slowly seeping through the top. He screeched to a halt from a dead run, his tail went up, he froze, and he turned.

It was lovely—it was so clear that his nose said to him, 'That's the smell!' and that his nose stopped him even when his feet wanted to keep going."

By the time the fish pipe was no longer needed to show Solo that the search was beginning, it had served its purpose. For Solo, Fish had forever bonded the concept of play to the scent of the deceased.

•   •   •   •   •   •   •   •   •   •

I had one small problem: I was rewarding Solo for doing something I didn't know much about.

Solo was getting better and better at telling me he had found teeth or a twist of cloth with a whiff of human remains scent on it.

I had questions. What compounds or chemicals were in that cloth or in that wisdom tooth that stopped Solo in his tracks? What was the history of cadaver-dog work? What did advanced training look like?

What else did I need to know in the many months or years before we might go on a search?

Solo is good at nose work. I'm good at bookwork.

I snuck into the veterinary college's library at my university. I'd never been there, and I found myself tiptoeing down the aisles, hoping no one would notice me.

Sure, I was a professor at this university, but veterinary medicine wasn't my territory. I was looking for a book that might help me and Solo find dead people.

There it was. The vet school had filed it under "social and public welfare and criminology." Its Library of Congress classification was HV8025 .R43 2000. The number two thousand stood for the year it was published.

I pulled the slender book out of the stacks. Andrew Rebmann was the first author. The cover photograph was odd. The German shepherd looked ordinary, but the guy behind the dog wore a getup that looked like he was about to work on a beehive. But the helmet and veil were black instead of white. And I knew that bees hate black. He also had disposable rubber gloves on. I realized that he was probably protecting himself from insects of other varieties. Like biting flies.

And the gloves? I could guess. I had seen enough crime shows.

I e-mailed Nancy to confess: "I borrowed the *Cadaver Dog Handbook* from the vet library."

I felt better when Nancy gave me only a brief lecture before noting her approval: "Remember, I warned you about being too brain-oriented. The Andy Rebmann book is good, though—he's the guru."

I opened the handbook

CADAVER DOG HANDBOOK

Forensic Training and Tactics for the Recovery of Human Remains

Andrew Rebmann
Edward David
Marcella H. Sorg

to the dedication page. A portion of it read: "To Clem (who didn't like dead people) and Rufus (who did)."

• • • • • • • • • • •

Andy Rebmann has trained and handled dogs for decades. Since he retired as a law enforcement dog handler and trainer in Connecticut, he's taught across the world. He's trained dogs and their handlers to track and trail criminals and lost people, to find narcotics and explosives. He's even trained dogs to help figure out how and where a fire might have started, especially if it was arson.

But cadaver-dog work has been his specialty for decades.

Andy was a young state trooper when he decided he wanted a patrol dog to be his partner. Patrol dogs do a bunch of things—trail criminals and find illegal drugs, for instance. But one of their main jobs is to protect their handler. Rufus, a German shepherd, was good at that. That was in 1972.

About a year later Andy also got a bloodhound, Tina. He fell in love with her nose and her trailing ability. Yet Andy noted that Tina had an irritating trait. If she was tracking someone and realized they were no longer alive, she would stop, looking puzzled and worried.

Even Clem, Andy's second bloodhound—who got a national award for his tracking and who was quite capable of biting a violent suspect if needed—was a coward when it came to finding bodies.

Like Tina, Clem refused to trail all the way to someone who was dead. The one time he did, he turned around and ran out the same way he'd come in.

"He almost turned me upside down," Andy said. "No way he was going to stay and sniff that guy."

This meant that on some cases Andy had to tie one of his bloodhounds to a tree and go poking around in the heavy brush himself. It was annoying.

Not long after that, Andy was at a conference when a

Photo courtesy of Andy Rebmann

Clem was nationally famous for finding people who were alive. He turned tail if they were dead.

New York state trooper, Ralph Suffolk, gave a presentation on something called "body dogs." Andy was fascinated.

He started thinking about Clem and Tina, and how much they hated finding bodies. He decided that what he needed was a body dog.

• • • • • • • • • • • •

So what do dead people smell like? Andy soon realized it was complicated. Just like people are complicated. Although death has been around as long as we have, only a few researchers today know much about the exact chemicals and compounds that are released after someone dies.

And in the mid-1970s, much less was known. But if Andy was going to train his dogs to find dead people and then train other handlers to train their dogs, he wanted to know more.

For most modern scientists and chemists, *odor mortis*—a Latin phrase for "smell of death"—is a new frontier. So even today, though a few scientists are getting closer, no one knows exactly what the dogs are smelling. We can't ask the dogs, and they can't tell us. They can only try their best to show us.

Most likely they are smelling a lot of things mixed together, especially if they are finding an entire body. But sometimes, like with a simple tooth or a dry bone, they may be smelling only a few compounds. One forensic scientist thinks more than one thousand compounds

USING SCIENCE TO SOLVE MYSTERIES

Forensic scientists use scientific methods and processes to solve crimes.

Sherlock Holmes, though fictional, might be considered one of the first forensic scientists! Today forensic scientists help solve all kinds of mysteries. They use their knowledge to help investigators, detectives, and juries understand what took place at a crime scene.

• Forensic chemists look at evidence such as DNA, fingerprints, hair, and fabric.

• Forensic toxicologists study how someone might have been poisoned or overdosed.

• Forensic anthropologists analyze decomposing and skeletal human remains.

may be associated with human decomposition.

The things we humans have invented—bombs, manufactured drugs, and land mines—are chemically simple in comparison with our own bodies.

Early on Andy thought decomposing animals and decomposing people probably smelled pretty much the same. That makes a lot of sense. We are, after all, mammals. Soon enough, though, Andy realized there were important differences.

Ideally you want to train dogs with the exact thing you want them to find out in the woods and fields, or in a warehouse. Especially because dead animals are common in both places.

Because Andy was a state trooper, his job gave him access to murder, accident, and suicide scenes. Once the

Photo by US Air Force Sergeant Shane A. Cuomo

A forensic anthropologist searches for bones
of servicemen lost in World War II.

forensic teams were done getting all the information they
needed, often something remained that Andy realized
could help train dogs.

For instance, like the woman in the Appalachian
Mountains who helped provide Solo with the material in
his fish pipe, crime or suicide scenes often have decomposition liquids in the surrounding dirt, or on sheets or
clothes that can be used for cadaver-dog training.

Andy still had one final thing he needed to do—find a
body-dog candidate. He knew the bloodhounds wouldn't
want to apply.

But he realized he already had a great candidate living
in his own house.

Rufus, Andy's stocky, dark German shepherd patrol dog, had started out as a potential guide dog for the blind at the Fidelco Guide Dog Foundation in Bloomfield, Connecticut. Rufus had flunked out of the program because he wasn't suited to calmly and gently guide anyone.

But Rufus was a fine patrol dog. And Andy started training him to find the dead.

That was in 1977, the same year Andy's bloodhound Clem won the award for being the best trailing dog in the nation.

Andy's first body dog, Rufus, was also his patrol K9.

Photo courtesy of Andy Rebmann

I finally understood what the mysterious dedication in the *Cadaver Dog Handbook* meant: "To Clem (who didn't like dead people) and Rufus (who did)."

As long as people were alive, Clem was happy to find them. If they were assumed to be dead? Rufus took over. It was a super deal for both dogs. Each got to do work he loved and was good at.

Cadaver dogs were first called body dogs. Which is descriptive. Because that's why they do, find bodies. But early on, journalists sometimes got the facts a little confused.

One newspaper reporter noted, with great sincerity and inaccuracy, that Rufus was "one of eight 'dead dogs' in the country; the only one in New England."

Such reports of Rufus's death were premature. He recovered twenty-six bodies in his career.

CHAPTER EIGHT

• • • • • • • • • • •

SEESAWS

I love to read and do research. But I also had another kind of homework to do. Homework I couldn't put off.

Nancy was teaching Solo to recognize the scent of human remains. I needed to teach Solo how to search for that scent. At this point it was easy for him to stick his head in a bucket and get a reward or even find his Fish in the backyard of our house in Durham.

It was time for Solo to learn how to go anywhere to find that scent—and not get distracted or decide an obstacle was too hard. It's also easier for dogs to learn challenging new material while they are young.

One good way to teach dogs has a lot in common with how you teach people a new skill. We call it "hands-on learning" for humans. For dogs let's call it "paws-on learning." You guide them a bit and keep them safe but allow them to learn as much as possible by themselves without becoming frustrated and quitting.

Search dogs need to be independent and brave, instead of constantly looking to the handler for what to do. I was starting to understand why some working-dog trainers liked dogs who were pains in the rear—the kinds of dogs who destroyed crates, who tore up the insides of cars, who challenged everything, who tried to jam three toys into their mouths at once. They were tough, and I needed to encourage Solo's toughness. When he found himself hesitating before crossing a creek, instead of making sad cooing sounds, I said in a bright voice, "Let's go! Good boy!"

I needed to keep my lips zipped while he learned to tolerate the scrape of a fence as he scrambled under it; to push through thick, thorny brush; and to swim across shallow rivers if the scent pulled him there. He had to know how to climb over dikes and crawl through large culverts. He needed to stop before tumbling over a cliff or trying to leap over a cattle guard. Even if it was snowing, or raining, or dark, he needed to learn to push through.

Then there were animal distractions. Solo needed to be respectful of the venomous copperhead snake sunning itself in the pine needles and to give the large snapping turtle space. He needed to learn to ignore rabbits and deer.

But learning those lessons doesn't happen all at once. They are learned best as puppy steps.

We had to teach Solo how to move about in the woods and fields—and rivers—with confidence. Here he learns how to swim in the Eno River.

David and I took Solo to the Eno River, a sleepy, shallow river in midsummer. I let Solo peer over the small cliff—after all, it wasn't the Grand Canyon—and then find his own spot where he could scramble down and wade in.

I kept myself, and David, contained. I remembered Nancy's words: "Stop chattering at him."

I threw his toy into the water where it was calm and knee high. He moved cautiously at first. Then he pounced like Tigger, spraying water everywhere.

Over the next few weeks we exposed Solo to some of Nancy's chickens doing their herky-jerky insect dance in the yard.

What was going to be the hardest for Solo was to learn

to ignore other dogs. That would take more time, but we had a good dog to practice with. Whiskey. Solo hated Whiskey, and Whiskey returned the compliment. They would run along opposite sides of a cyclone fence, snarling at

Solo needed to be exposed to all sorts of distractions that he might run into on a search, like chickens.

each other. So we kept Solo a little farther away, where he knew Whiskey was there but not a direct threat.

I was a distraction too, with my clumsiness. I taught Solo to teeter on a low balance beam in the backyard and to keep his paws on the board. When I tried to reward him and throw his toy, I botched it. He managed to grab the toy and my thumb. I didn't make a single bleat of pain.

Teaching him to not be a wimp helped me not be a wimp. I had to be a good role model.

• • • • • • • • • • •

A dog becoming expert at something is like you or your friend becoming a good chess player or turning into an agile gymnast by the time you are in middle school. Working-dog trainers have no doubt that dogs become good at certain tasks the more they train. And trainers aren't worried about whether a dog's learning mimics a human's, as long as the dog learns, keeps learning, and then layers that knowledge.

Solo ultimately needed to be like a gymnast, agile and physically fit, while using his nose for increasingly complex scent problems. That dexterity and multitasking is what one researcher calls "canine expertise."

William "Deak" Helton believes that dogs can be experts. They just can't tell you about it directly.

"Although canine experts cannot verbalize their knowledge, this in no way implies they do not have it," he wrote.

We humans sometimes forget that dogs have learning curves like us. It takes time to hone search and sniffing skills. It wasn't like I was an expert at searching. I'd have to leave the sniffing up to Solo.

I vowed to give us both a chance, even if he wasn't giving my fingers much of one.

Science aside, good dog trainers are clear about the order of things. You break things down into small steps. Solo needed to learn to swim before I placed some teeth or a piece of sheet with the scent of human remains across the river for him and expected him to forge the river. He needed to learn to ignore the chickens before I asked him to search with them clucking a few yards away.

Photo courtesy of Nancy Hook

Whiskey, Nancy's German shepherd, loved to bait Solo.

It's a lot like building a house. You lay the foundation first, and then you can start building up. If the foundation isn't solid and level, nothing you build on top will hold.

If I rushed the order of things, I'd be left with a shaky, unreliable dog.

. . . .

Something strange and wonderful happened while we were taking Solo to the river and to Home Depot and to Nancy's. One night in early winter, I realized what it was. I forgot that he was an impossible brat king. That manic energy, which made me so nervous when we first got him, was being channeled and directed. We all slept soundly at night.

Solo was growing up, occasionally acting like an adult shepherd!

In early January, David and I headed to the beach, with friends and dogs all piled into a rented SUV. I wasn't dreaming about romantic sunset walks on the beach with David. I had started seeing the North Carolina landscape as one endless opportunity to train Solo. As David drove, I stared out the window at loblolly pine plantations and abandoned concrete-block buildings. Could we train there? Would the landowners let us? That long-harvested soy field looked like a promising place to stash a cadaver-training aid. I now had material other than the tooth and the fish pipe to help Solo learn the scent of the deceased.

Even bitter winter wind and prickly pear cactus hidden in the sand at Kill Devil Hills sounded like fun to me—a great way to challenge Solo in a new environment.

Solo learned to find his training material at the beach, in the garbage can at the end of the driveway of our rental house, in the backyard sand, amid a patch of prickly pear. I was elated as I wrote my training reports.

On the second night at the beach, I called Dad in Oregon to check in and tell him about our impromptu vacation. I told him I would send him pictures of his Megan, who had been running blissfully up and down the beaches, a maroon-colored wraith in the winter fog. Dad sounded dreadful; his voice was thick and slow. His hip had been hurting the last six months, since shortly after he had visited us in North Carolina. His doctor had thought it was a side effect of a medication he took, but it hadn't gotten better. I got off the phone and started to cry. David and my friends gathered around me, gently comforting me as I sobbed.

Perhaps somewhere deep down, I knew.

I had never said much to Dad about training Solo to find missing people. I didn't know why, exactly. He was a fisheries and wildlife biologist, so he would have understood the science of it.

But he was also a university professor, and what I was doing with Solo went beyond reading the wind and understanding decomposition and scent patterns. It might put me back into the world that Dad found dangerous. I didn't want him to worry about me.

Part of it was that he didn't fully understand my odd love of dogs like Solo. He preferred female setters who draped themselves on him, placing their paws on the sleeves of his old sweaters, pulling the wool threads gently and insistently with their untrimmed nails.

When he called me a few days later, David and I and the dogs were home from the beach. I was oddly unsurprised that Dad finally had a diagnosis. Cancer.

I was shocked at how far along it was.

I stopped training Solo. I left David alone with the dogs and flew from North Carolina to Oregon to spend a few precious remaining weeks with Dad.

Dad died seven weeks after that phone call at the beach.

The world felt cold and dreary to me without my father.

Afterward, I took long walks across the meadows near his home, missing David and the dogs. But mostly I missed my father. I was a grown-up, but I wasn't sure how to move forward without him.

CHAPTER NINE

· · · · · · · · · · ·

CAROLINA COW PIES

Solo had missed me when I flew to Oregon to see Dad. When I came back, exhausted and sad, he didn't provide quiet comfort. Instead he howled in joy, tried to use my legs as an obstacle course to weave through, dashed off to find a toy, and shoved it at my midsection. Play. Outside. Now.

He was a year old and looked like a powerful young velociraptor—his head too big for his body, his tail like a large thrashing rudder.

He had zero interest in my grief. If I stared at him vacantly, wishing I could call Dad, that was Solo's cue to demand a game of tug.

Solo's obedience training suffered slightly in my

absence, but he and Megan were now true companions.

While I was gone, Megan had trained Solo to play in a way I couldn't have imagined him capable of with another dog. He was subtle, light on his feet. Nothing rowdy. Megan didn't believe in contact sports.

I thought about my options. I could continue to mope. Or I could contact Nancy Hook.

She was sympathetic and practical.

"You really liked your father. Come on out and bring Solo to train."

That's what I did.

I had missed an entire season at Nancy's farm. When

Photo by Cat Warren

Megan and Solo had become good friends.

Nancy and Solo made me go outside and play.

we were there last, it wore the tans and grays and browns of early winter, though undershoots of green lurk year-round in North Carolina.

Nancy had exchanged her winter canvas pants for her light camo pants stuffed into tall rubber boots. Her copper-red hair was covered with a baseball cap instead of a wool knit cap. Otherwise, she hadn't changed. She had become one of my measuring sticks for what was normal—her laughter, her ease, her balance.

It was hard to grieve in the midst of a soft Carolina spring.

I had to watch my feet and control Solo, who now always worked off lead so he could follow scent. I had to keep him away from Whiskey's fence, away from the chickens running around and sounding an alarm:

Kuh-kuh-kuh-kack! Shepherd on the loose! We had to avoid Rocky, Nancy's chestnut horse, with his massive hooves. He didn't allow dogs to take liberties.

Scariest of all were the Hereford cows with their new calves, scattered across the muddy green fields. Solo lowered his body to stalk them. That would not end well. The protective mammas were not going to tolerate shepherd high jinks.

"Solo!" I cried.

Nancy laughed. "Get that high, panicky tone out of your voice."

I got the squeak out of my voice and told Solo to come. My voice was an octave lower. I sounded like I meant it.

It worked. He reluctantly swung back toward me, and I leashed him up until we got farther down the field, away from the cows.

I freed him again. He wanted to make it clear that he'd won the canine-cow face-off, so he sauntered over to lift his leg on an electric fence.

We could hear the *bzzt* of electricity from twenty yards away. He didn't flinch. That, Nancy told me, is exactly what you want in a cadaver dog. If he could ignore that jolt, nothing would shut him down.

* * * * * * * * * * * *

I didn't shut down either. I trained Solo several times a week. I found new places to train near our house. Now when I put cadaver-training aids out in glass jars, I walked a different way into the area, downwind, to hide the jars in a direction I knew I wouldn't start him for the search itself.

He was clever, and I didn't want him to use my scent, carried directly to him on the wind, or my footsteps as a shortcut to finding what I'd hidden. I wanted the scent of the hide itself to be his only cue.

I put the hides out at our local feed-and-seed warehouse, which had pigeon poop and running mice. Solo was less distracted than I was.

Each time I trained him, I kept a record, based on a template from the *Cadaver Dog Handbook*. What time did we start? What was the temperature and humidity? What was the wind doing? Coming from the northeast or east? How many miles per hour?

Most important of all—what mistakes did either of us make?

My training records showed how far we needed to go. Solo needed a better alert on one hide. A barking dog distracted him on a second. I put his hide in too difficult a spot on a third, setting him up for failure. I didn't reward him long enough on a fourth.

Instead of a sit-and-whine for his alert, we changed to a down-and-whine alert. Then Solo decided he didn't want to whine. After that, he decided he hated lying down.

We transferred to a rubber Kong toy for his reward. Solo wouldn't give it back. He refused to search next to the dog lot if Whiskey was there. He stared at the cows and

CADAVER DOG TRAINING RECORD -- SOLO and CAT WARREN

Date of training: June 16, 2005

Training Location: Norton St. Durham

Terrain (type): large abandoned house ready for demolition on 2-acre lot that has been recently cleared with piles of brush, slight undergrowth.

Time problem set: 45 minutes ahead

Time Solo started work: 7:35 p.m.

Time involved in search: 5 minutes; 1 minutes; 5 minutes

Weather Conditions: sunny

Wind Direction: calm, northwest

Wind Speed: minimal

Temperature: 77 degrees

Other: 62 percent humidity

Type of training aid: pvc pipe, two baggies of dried cadaver material

Type of problem(s) (describe): Husband hid baggies and PVC pipe in three locations on about a 2-acre spread with handler not knowing where: two slightly buried piles of brush cleared on lot; one in crotch of tree about 7 feet up.

Training Aid Located? Yes (X)   No ( )

Comments/Criticisms on Solo's/Handler's Work:
Solo found all three hides with good consistent down as alert. His give is terrible on the Kong; doesn't want to return it. Flushed a rabbit, but got immediately back to work, not even chasing it much (he was working on harness, but didn't even go to end of harness before turning back to work). His stiffening and tail movement is getting more obvious on his alerts; he doesn't whine. Very solid searching this time with little distraction from other dog scents, etc. Worked around edge of house as well, but showed no interest.

Date of Report: 06/16/05   **Signature:**

thought about how much fun it would be to chase them. Nancy reminded me to keep my voice low and forceful.

Solo's being a singleton kept raising its ugly head. Except for Megan and two or three neighborhood exceptions, he despised dogs his own size.

One day during training, a stray—a female Labrador mix—came running and wagging and crawling across the field while we were training. Solo flashed his teeth and rolled her repeatedly.

Then he attacked Wolfie, the German shepherd search dog he should have been cooperating with.

He didn't like small dogs either. Nancy rescued Boston terriers who had been mistreated or abandoned. I had to rescue one of them from Solo. Solo lunged, the grass was wet, my foot slipped, my voice skyrocketed into high soprano again.

These moments made me despair and Nancy shrug. Solo hadn't killed tough little Yankee. He'd just considered it.

"Blast, blast, blast," Joan wrote me after I described how unprepared I was for Solo's reactions. "Aggression and the canine mind are so very interesting . . . and sad, when it is your dog. The one thing I can say is that if he wanted to do harm, he could and would have. So, as nasty as these incidents are, he doesn't appear to be hurting dogs physically."

She was right. Solo was all teeth and hackles and growls. He never drew blood.

That didn't comfort me. I took him back to obedience classes. I worked on my timing, watching closely so that I could break his hard stare with another dog by blocking his view with my body. It helped de-escalate the tension. I communicated a clear, consistent message: Don't be a teenage bully. No one likes them.

The work started to pay off. We survived the Night of the Snapping Fox Terrier without even a growl on Solo's part. We got through the happy-pit-bull-on-top-of-the-shepherd incident without a single tooth hitting skin.

David and I knew Solo would never be entirely relaxed with dogs other than Megan. Yet he responded to us more and more. He was no less energetic, but he was becoming our friend. To our great relief, he liked humans, including babies and children.

At night he gazed at us steadily with his dark caramel eyes, and occasionally even lay his oversize head on our laps and fell asleep without demanding yet another game.

• • • • • • • • • •

Nancy was making our training problems harder and harder. Before I knew it, it was midsummer. Solo was fifteen months old.

Solo despised other dogs, but he found
small humans fascinating.

AMAZING EVERYDAY ARTHROPODS

Nineteen species of dragonflies and damselflies live in North Carolina. A dragonfly is the fastest flying insect known. Some can go thirty-five miles per hour. And they can fly backward!

• Sulphur butterflies, named after the bright yellow chemical, are common throughout North Carolina. They love blooming clover, cow pies—and corpses.

• Japanese beetles are a glorious metallic green and bronze. In their native Japan, natural predators keep their numbers down. Not here. In the US they can destroy three hundred species of plants and trees, making leaves look like skeletons.

• If Solo and I had been out at twilight, we might have seen big dipper fireflies sending flashing coded messages to find a mate. Their flight looks like the familiar constellation. Their luminescent rear ends light as they fly upward in an arc.

• Assassin bugs use a beak to inject venom into their prey. Then they wait briefly for their victim's internal organs to turn liquid—and drink the delicious juice. Farmers love them because they dine on insects that eat crops. The wheel bug is the largest assassin bug in North Carolina.

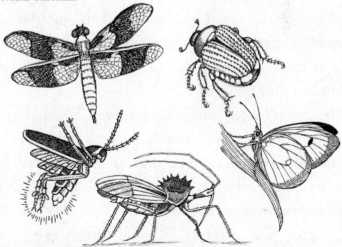

We stood at the top of a large cow pasture north of Nancy's house. Common whitetail dragonflies, looking like pieces of chalk on the wing, buzzed across clumps of grass to land on fresh cow pies.

It was hot and humid. The cows were hanging out at the bottom of the field, on the far side of the cool swamp and pond. Their babies were grown and gone.

Solo whined as I held him. I threw a little handful of grass up to find which direction the wind was coming from, so it could help us on the search by bringing scent toward us. The grass fell limply to the ground. The moist air barely moved.

"Find the Fish!" I said. As I unclipped his lead and Solo pushed away from me, Nancy narrowed her eyes and looked at me. She twisted her fingers next to her lips and threw away the invisible key.

I knew what she meant. No chatter.

One field stretched out in front of us, and then one beyond that. I'd worked them before with Solo. But Nancy had purposely started forgetting where she planted some of the training materials.

She was also teaching me how to walk a Z search pattern by fixing on spots on the horizon, so that Solo and I didn't miss an area. I told her that I'd use the big "deciduous tree" on the hill as one marker. She laughed at my snobby tree vocabulary.

After a few minutes of zigging and zagging, Solo ignored my pattern. He threw his head up. He'd caught a whiff of cadaver scent. He ran downhill, straight into the cow-pie-filled swamp.

He slowed, his tail stiffened into the piggy loop that now let me know he was near cadaver-training material, and he lay down in the muck, staring silently at me.

His new alert.

"Throw it. Quick!" Nancy yelled from the top of the hill.

I clumsily pulled the Kong on a rope out of my pocket and tossed it to Solo, who lunged out of the muck with a sucking sound.

Nancy gathered up the muddy jar. That wasn't the only hide out there. She swept her hand up and across the pasture in a big, vague wave.

The next one could be anywhere. It was hotter out. Solo sniffed and ran and panted. He wasn't getting a whiff of anything.

Nancy criticized my search pattern. Too much zig. Not enough zag. I wanted to give Solo some water from his new water bag.

She reminded me that we hadn't been working that long, and it wasn't that hot out. I gave him water anyway. It gave me a chance to catch my breath.

I restarted the search, though it seemed hopeless. "Find your Fish!" I trudged back and forth, back and forth.

Then Solo's head went down. He slowed more, plunging his nose deep along a high ridge of grass.

He moved away from me fast, heading along the ridge. When he was about thirty feet away, he stiffened and

Solo searching for training material in a
large cow pasture next to Nancy's house.

circled. Then he was down, bam. Right next to a cow pie,
nails dug hard into the ground.

He stared at me.

I moved fast and flung the Kong before Nancy could
yell at me.

Solo growled in joy and tossed the Kong for himself,
bouncing it off his nose.

Nancy walked over and lifted the dried cow pie that
was the size of a large dinner plate. Underneath was a dry
bone. It looked like a small beef spare rib.

It was a donation from a friend and fellow dog trainer
Nancy knew. He had a rib removed during surgery and
didn't want it to go to waste.

Nancy looked at Solo. She looked at me. She shook her
head in disbelief.

CHAPTER TEN

. . . .

LIBERTY WAREHOUSE

I wanted to keep at least a few steps ahead of Solo, and that meant I needed to find more places to train and more people to train with. Nancy told me about a death investigator who worked at the medical examiner's office. Lisa Mayhew helped train detectives to collect and preserve evidence when someone has died, and no one yet knows whether it's an accident or murder.

Lisa also had a cadaver dog.

Nancy didn't have her e-mail, but I knew where to look. Solo and I needed more help to find people out in the woods. But I'm good at finding people on the Web.

From: Cat Warren
Sent: Thursday, August 25, 4:53 PM
To: Lisa Mayhew
I have the funny feeling, having searched the net compulsively while Nancy Hook is off to a seminar this weekend and sending only cryptic e-mails my way (it's felt like a scavenger hunt), that you may be the Lisa I'm looking for—with a German shorthaired pointer who does Search and Rescue.

From: Lisa Mayhew
Sent: Thursday, August 25, 10:31 PM
To: Cat Warren
You found the right Lisa! There is a seminar being held in Rockingham County that my team is putting on. We do two a year. I can let my captain know you may be coming.

It was that easy. I started training with a group of search-and-rescue and cadaver-dog handlers from the foothills of North Carolina.

Solo knew what it meant when I woke up before dawn and took out the pants and hiking boots I wore for training. He whined and paced as I dressed and stumbled downstairs.

Dogs live mostly in the present, something humans are bad at. Human minds often scurry straight to the future. Distracted, we miss what is happening in the here and now.

Solo possessed both dog and human senses of time.

He loved the present, but he was a whiz at anticipating future fun.

As David made coffee and I brought in the newspapers, Solo dashed from the bedroom to the front door, from the yard to the car, and then back to the house. The sky turned pearly gray.

Stop dawdling. Outside is better than inside. Let's go!

We'd be on the road by six a.m., just as the horizon started to lighten with pale streaks. I drove on back roads toward the foothills.

Solo and I were soon in the company of howling bloodhounds and men and women in camouflage. I liked them a lot. They tolerated me, and they taught me. I learned to appreciate country ham and biscuits and Dunkin' Donuts coffee for breakfast.

Ken Young—with his military bearing, his trimmed mustache and sly smile that hovered beneath his olive fatigue cap, and a pistol strapped at his side—ran a florist shop.

On weekends he ran dogs and people. He gave directions to a group of slouching handlers in the firehouse, many of them with plugs of tobacco tucked inside their lower lips. I didn't chew tobacco. I tried to slouch.

Ken warned everyone about the dangers in the woods, the need to pay attention to what other people and dogs were doing. Mostly, he said, don't do anything stupid.

Then he would give that trademark smile. "Let's go have some fun out there."

We did.

While I told Solo to find his Fish, some of the cadaver-dog handlers from the foothills told their dogs to "Find napoo." It was an evocative and mysterious command. The handlers told me it was a Navajo term for the dead. The term seemed to have spread far beyond the Southwest, where the Native American tribe mostly lived. In the cadaver-dog world, the word "napoo" went as far north as Canada and as far east as North Carolina.

I looked it up. "Napoo" wasn't Navajo. It was British military slang for "death," from World War I. It probably came from the French phrase *Il n'y en a plus.* "There is no more."

It doesn't matter what you tell your dog. You could say, "It's Groundhog Day!" Or "What's up, Doc?"

As long as the dog learns to associate those particular words with finding those odd smells you want him to look for, all is well.

Dogs are so good at reading clues we give out unconsciously that words are usually beside the point. By the time we started training, the sun had risen, and Solo was ready. He whirled and twirled with joy.

He didn't need to hear the words "Find the Fish." He knew, as Sherlock Holmes said to Dr. Watson, "Come, Watson, come! The game is afoot!"

. . . .

I didn't have much spare time, but training and working with Solo every weekend, and often during the week, made me feel like I was back in my rural 4-H club as a twelve-year-old.

The 4-H pledge covered it all. When I worked with Solo, I pledged "my head," "my heart," "my hands," and "my health." I had to. He was big, he was smart, and he learned in leaps and bounds.

And there were lots of new practical matters to attend to. I needed to find more cadaver-dog training material.

Darlene Griffin, who handled bloodhound cadaver dogs like Lucky, helped train me and Solo.

The wisdom tooth of Nancy's now-ex-husband, the rib, and the twist of cloth in the fish pipe were only the beginning. Solo needed a variety of scent materials to train on, from fresh to older to ancient. The material he trained on needed to mimic what he might find buried in the woods or in an abandoned building on a real search.

So in the midst of answering student e-mails at my university office, I'd find myself googling. I ordered a search-and-rescue-dog package of human bones from the Bone Room in California—although I called the state medical examiner's office first to make sure that North Carolina allowed it. Each state has different rules about what kind of cadaver-training material you can store and use.

I was delighted when the order arrived in the mailbox, a small cardboard box with an ivory fibula and some toe bones in a plastic bag. The foot bones looked remarkably like the foam peanuts they came nestled in.

When I had my teeth cleaned, I talked with my dentist about how to get a couple of molars or wisdom teeth for training. He was happy to provide a few from patients who no longer needed them. He was fascinated that dogs might be able to smell older bones. He lent me, briefly, the jawbone from an anatomical teaching skull that had been in his office for decades. He and I wanted to see whether Solo could find it.

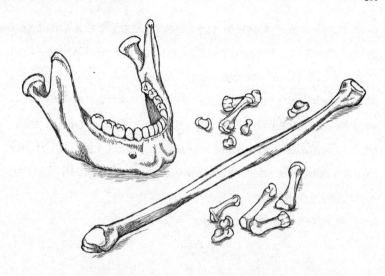

**Although old, dry bones have little scent,
a well-trained dog can find them.**

Solo found the jawbone, though he looked surprised when he put his nose next to it. He was underwhelmed. That's it? I reacted to that bit of scent?

I rewarded him with great enthusiasm. Yes, indeed! That IS it! Good boy! Good Fish!

I reported the outcome to my dentist when I returned his teaching jawbone.

Lisa Mayhew helped too. One warm summer evening the two of us cut up an old bedsheet for training aids. It had lain for days underneath an undiscovered body in an apartment. It smelled gross, but we were both used to it. It had plenty of decomposition scent for Solo's training. We didn't need the whole thing—just six-inch-by-six-inch patches that we popped into mason jars. We knelt in front of our bounty to make careful cuts, then rocked back on our heels. We had to make sure our double-rubber-gloved hands didn't touch anything except the material. The scissors would have to be carefully disposed of. We didn't want to accidentally contaminate ourselves or the jars with any human remains scent. We smiled. Solo whined in the car, waiting for training.

It was a beautiful evening.

●　●　●　●　●　●　●　●　●　●　●

Before I knew it, Solo turned two.

I knew that taking my and Solo's training to the next level over the coming year might throw our comfortable routine out the window. But if I were ever going to use Solo in an actual search, it was time to get certified as a cadaver-dog team. That meant taking tests. That made me realize, nervously, how much I didn't know.

I needed to up my game, to "bond with the badge." That is, I needed to find a way to work with the police. They often, though not always, know if someone is missing and perhaps dead. If my first goal—certifying Solo—was uncertain, my second goal—getting access to the world of law enforcement—was like winning the lottery.

Once again Lisa Mayhew helped. She knew a fine police K9 trainer who happened to work in Durham. He was in charge of the Durham Police K9 unit.

It took me an hour to compose the brief e-mail to

Sergeant Mike Baker, asking whether we might meet.

"Sgt. Baker," my e-mail began. I made my tone formal, respectful. No humor.

Solo and I, I wrote, "have been training fairly steadily since he was eight months old."

"Fairly steadily" was fairly accurate. I set Solo's training aside for just three months when Dad died. It felt like so much longer.

I waited. Five long days.

Mike Baker e-mailed back, apologizing for the delay. He'd been out of town.

From: Baker, Mike
Sent: Wednesday, June 28, 9:50 p.m.
Re: a cadaver dog in training
To: Cat Warren
Hi, Cat. My specialty is in law enforcement dogs, but many
of the same theories/principles apply to what you do. If
nothing else, I'm sure we could expose Solo to new training
areas and obstacles.
Take care,
Mike

Mike followed through on his promise to expose Solo and me to new training. "Meet us at the old Liberty tobacco warehouse at eight p.m.," he said. So what if it hit ninety-five degrees at three p.m.? That's ideal North Carolina dog-training weather.

I, on the other hand, have asthma that gets triggered by days on end of code-orange polluted air. I also like to be in bed by ten.

I dressed and re-dressed myself that night. I settled on a white T-shirt tucked into khaki cargo pants. Then I tried the shirt outside the pants to see if it looked more natural. It looked sloppy. I tucked it back into the pants. I

Photo by Allison Marchant

Liberty warehouse was one of the last surviving auction houses for tobacco.

tousled my moussed hair a little, trying to create a natural cool. But it was hot, and I was sweaty. My hair stood up in spikes.

The mousse melted and dripped into my eyes, making them sting. I scrubbed at my eyes and looked at the warehouse in front of me. It was one of the last standing auction houses for loose-leaf tobacco, once the economic spine of Durham.

Now the warehouse leaked during rainstorms. It was covered with metal siding. The owners had boarded over most of the natural skylights that once let buyers see the color of the bright leaf tobacco, so they could bid on prices.

From the outside I saw the sloping floors that tobacco farmers once drove their wagons down. Huge beams reached up into darkness.

I took a deep breath and walked down the slope, into the heart of the warehouse.

CHAPTER ELEVEN

. . . .

AN ANCHOR ON A LEASH

In front of me I saw a group of men in navy T-shirts and cargo pants standing, arms folded across chests, in a loose circle around a pickup truck.

I looked more closely. Not all men. Two women. I felt some relief. They all silently watched a dog and handler work. The dog, a fawn-colored Belgian Malinois, looked like a shorthaired, sharp-nosed German shepherd with a rattail. His tail stiff, the dog slowly circled a pickup that was parked just inside the warehouse entrance.

He sniffed as he circled, the tires, the wheel wells, along the truck's side and underbelly. At the back he froze, nose inches from the license plate. He leaped like a cat, straight onto the open pickup bed. Then he wheeled and anchored his nose to the top of the license plate. It was as though an invisible magnet kept his nose in place while the rest of his body continued to spin around it.

I heard a low, gentle chuckle. Someone breathed out slowly, "Good dog. Good dog!" A tennis ball flipped through the air, landed in front of that anchored nose, and bounced.

Game on.

The dog's nails scrabbled for purchase on the concrete as he chased the ball through the powdered tobacco-leaf dust.

I knew who Mike Baker was because of the way he assessed the dog's work. And because I saw who threw the ball. Medium build, medium-short brown hair, medium Irish-English features—the kind of guy who might not stand out in a crowd of noisy dogs and macho cops. But as one handler who comes from another county to train says, "Mike's magic."

As the dog and handler trotted out of the warehouse back to their car, Mike nodded at me. I walked over, and we shook hands. Then I stood, my arms folded across my chest, as the next dog and handler came into the warehouse.

The Durham patrol dogs and their handlers show up for city events and school show-and-tells. Outside of this, they mostly work, answer calls, and train. That night I started to get used to the background sound of radio crackle. Even during training, one of the handler-and-dog teams needed to answer calls.

Durham has a sizable K9 unit. But not enough people go

Sgt. Mike Baker and police K9 handler Danny Gooch
work with Ren, using cardboard boxes to teach him
the scent of illegal drugs. It's here!

missing and are presumed dead for the police department
to spend money and time training their own dogs to do
cadaver-dog work. Durham police patrol dogs keep plenty
busy—searching for drugs, tracking suspects, responding
to reports of break-ins, and protecting their handlers.

It's like that around the country. The majority of
cadaver-dog work falls to volunteers—big teams, or indi-
vidual dogs and handlers like Solo and me.

I'd had little exposure to male trainers up to this point.
Women dominate the obedience and agility world and,
though to a lesser degree, the search-and-rescue seminar
world. Men tend to dominate the law-enforcement K9

world. That world tends to be a rougher place than the obedience world, where clickers and treats increasingly rule. In the working K9 world, square-chain choke collars are common and liver treats nonexistent.

But, at least in the Durham unit, any handler who forgot to take off the corrective choke collar and replace it with a leather collar or a harness was instantly reprimanded. And no one was allowed to take his or her temper out on the dog.

Working dogs need the same basic thing, whatever the gender of their handler. They need to hear high, cheery voices when they're being rewarded. They need to get their reward at the right moment. And they need lots of play.

"Make it fun for him," Mike counseled a too-serious, alto-voiced handler. Mike modeled the behavior he wanted: "Pump him up. Attaboy, attaboy, attaboy!" He pitched his own voice ever skyward into a soprano croon.

Solo and I got our chance to train at nine-thirty p.m. Close to my bedtime. The temperature outside the warehouse had dropped into the low nineties, but it was still nearly a hundred degrees inside. I didn't complain.

Mike turned to me and said the even, quiet words that would become so familiar: "Why don't you go get your dog?"

• • • • • • • • • • • •

I could barely see Solo's bat-eared silhouette. He had fogged the inside windows of the car that I had kept running to keep him cool.

I remembered to walk him, so that he could pee before we entered the warehouse. That gave Solo the chance to realize the threat he faced. Patrol-dog urine coated the weeds up and down the block. Solo walked into the dark warehouse stiff-legged, his fur raised down his neck and spine, ready to face monsters.

The scent of all the excited Malinois and Dutch shepherds and German shepherds who trained before him floated through the air.

Solo and I blew the training. We weren't a team. I was trembling a bit, and I didn't have a search pattern. He kept shooting glances over his shoulder to see whether other dogs were stalking him. Then he finally started working, moving down the long rows of stacked planks in the rear of the warehouse. He easily found the hides Mike had placed—he slowed down, stiffened, and also got that little piggy crick in his tail.

Mike saw it too. But it takes more than Solo finding the training aids. He needed to tell me, and he needed to stay at that spot.

Solo went to each hide, sniffed, and then walked on. It was pathetic.

I can't remember if I made excuses. I'm sure I did. Mike was sympathetic but firm. He complimented Solo on his "work ethic" but explained what he wanted. I already knew.

Solo paid too much attention to me during the search. My own nervous scent must have been rolling off me in

Solo gets a distinctive twist to his tail
when he smells cadaver scent.

waves. I probably distracted him from his dog obsession. But I also distracted him from the job he was supposed to do.

It was a relief to put Solo back in the car and return to watch the other dogs. They found hidden handlers, acting as "decoys," or fake suspects, perched in the warehouse's massive rafters. The patrol dogs' deep warning barks rang out, along with their handlers' standard warnings. "Suspect in the building. This is Durham K9. Come out with your hands up. This is your final warning. Come out with your hands up, or I will send the dog."

No suspect appeared.

Released, the patrol dogs tracked the fake suspects, found them, and barked harshly and repeatedly until the handler arrived. Sometimes the decoy would throw the dog a toy reward—a Kong or tennis ball. That signaled the end of the exercise.

Other times, the decoy descended from the rafters, protected with a heavy padded "bite" sleeve, and threatened the handler. The dog, whose job was to protect his handler, launched, mouth gaping, with all four feet in the air, and slammed into the hard sleeve.

The dog was encouraged to hang on steadily while the decoy struggled, sweat mixing with tobacco dust and dog saliva.

"Praise him up," Mike told a handler, who ran his hand soothingly and approvingly over the muzzle of his dog, who was hanging on to the bite sleeve. That caress calmed the dog, helped him hold steadily and securely until he was told to let go. Sometimes the decoy would slip off the sleeve and give it to the dog as a final reward for his work, a big chew toy he could carry out of the warehouse.

I was fascinated. It took guts, nerves, and perfect timing on the part of all three players—the dog, the handler, and the decoy.

I stayed well out of the way.

• • • • • • • • • • •

Photo by Cat Warren

**Mike Baker, protected with a padded sleeve, acts
as a decoy for Wes Hawkins's K9, Tanner.**

"Figured you'd have some nerves and that would rattle
Solo a bit," Nancy said in her later e-mail to me. "It sounds
like you did pretty darn good, though, well enough to let
Mike know Solo is reliable. I know you can learn a lot
from those guys."

Mike e-mailed me too. He was fair in his criticism.
Break it down, he said. Worry about one building block at
a time. Don't try to control everything. Let Solo initiate
the game.

Of course I try to control everything. Now I had two trainers saying the same thing: let go.

I read and reread Mike's and Nancy's advice.

I also realized Solo might have an advantage here that he didn't have at the many puppy classes we flunked. K9 handlers don't expect their dogs to get along. Most of their dogs have a snarky edge.

Every dog was on lead until they started working. Each dog worked separately. The warehouse rang with other warnings I would become accustomed to: "Dog in!" or "Dog out!"

For me, those warnings were a comfort. I wouldn't have to keep my eyes peeled for a shorthaired pointer to come bounding over off lead.

Most important of all, Mike's training philosophy fit Solo's attitude to a T. "Remember," Mike wrote, "we are just anchors holding on to their leash."

. . . .

CHAPTER TWELVE

GOLDILOCKS AND THE THIRTEEN BEASTS

During that first warehouse training, I channeled Nancy's warning not to chatter at Solo. The same rule held for watching police K9 handlers work their dogs. I learned the value of keeping my mouth shut.

Mike Baker invited Solo and me back. Again. Then again. For one night every two weeks in summer and fall, and one afternoon every two weeks in winter and spring, I joined police K9 trainings.

I was nervous but happy. It felt like the beginning of something. I spent much of my time hanging back, studying. I was a student once more. In the vocabulary of the working-dog world, I was a "green" handler.

While Solo waited impatiently in the car for his turn, I

followed behind dogs and handlers as they ranged through deserted buildings or woods. Training had a rhythm defined by what most aroused the dogs, or tired them out.

The K9s usually worked on finding narcotics first while their noses were fresh, and they weren't panting hard. They then moved on to simple tracks, where they weren't looking for hidden "suspects" but for dropped articles. Then came searching for suspects.

I learned how each dog worked scent differently. Some used their noses low and deep. Others were opportunists, and held their heads higher and even cut corners to move more quickly. All the dogs captured live human scent from both the ground and the currents of air.

I watched inexperienced handlers become frustrated

During training, a K9 waits at the side of his handler for the cue to confront a suspect.

Photo by Cat Warren

as their dogs overran and then lost the direction the suspect had gone. Long lines got tangled in brambles and trees. I also witnessed those same handlers experience that moment of utter pride and triumph when their dogs learned to trail someone across hot asphalt, fields, and shallow creeks, never losing the person's scent.

And, as always, I listened, so that when it was time, I could easily hear Mike say to me, "Why don't you go get your dog?"

Solo had calmed from that first night. With cops and patrol cars around, he realized he could ignore sharp barks, growls, and dog-permeated air.

I no longer apologized for his personality. To police K9 handlers, Solo wasn't a jackass. He was just a dog.

· · · · · · · · · · · ·

The days and nights watching the K9 unit train made me appreciate two things: (1) how sensitive the dog's nose is, and (2) how adaptable dogs are to different kinds of searching, as they can locate the faint smell of illegal drugs or trail a suspect through busy streets.

But research scientists, who question everything until they can prove it with controlled experiments, have never assumed the dog's nose is superior to all other noses.

Some of the most interesting nose experiments happened during the 1970s. But scientists searched beyond the dog. They wanted to figure out which animal's nose worked best for a variety of tasks. Much of that research went on at a Texas institute founded and funded by a quirky millionaire.

Tom Slick Jr. was an oilman, an inventor, and a committed cryptozoologist—someone who believes in beasts that exist only in folklore. Though some real beasts come very close to fitting the criteria of what are called "cryptids." There's a very cool salamander in China that has reached more than five feet in length, for example. You don't have to turn to myth to find the miraculous in nature.

Slick spent years, and many millions of dollars, looking for the mysterious hairy snowman of the Himalayas, the yeti, and for its North American cousin, bigfoot, or Sasquatch. He searched for the Loch Ness Monster in Scotland.

He paid for three separate expeditions to Nepal to search for the yeti. Slick tried to get permission from the Nepalese government to use a helicopter and tracking bloodhounds to find the huge, imaginary snowman. But the country refused to let the dogs in. The dogs probably wouldn't have helped find something that didn't exist.

Slick's real contribution to science wasn't in his futile hunts for Nessie or bigfoot, but in founding several research institutes, including Southwest Research Institute near San Antonio, Texas, in 1947.

He filled the place with smart researchers who wanted to use engineering, science, and technology to solve practical problems.

And they didn't only focus on machines. In the early 1970s some of the scientists, working with military

A depiction of an imaginary yeti.
Slick spent years trying to find one in Nepal.

researchers, started thinking that animals—real ones—
might help humans solve some practical problems.

In that same era, the US role in the conflict in Vietnam
started winding down. Military researchers noticed what
dogs did during that long and brutal war.

Sentries or scout dogs warned soldiers of the enemy's
approach. Sometimes, they moved ahead of the troops
through the jungle.

Truffle hunter and her pig in France.

Woodcut, by Louis Malteste, 1893

They were used, less often, to detect the fine wire filaments stretched across jungle paths. Those wires triggered bombs. The dogs also helped soldiers detect punji pits, holes filled with sharp wooden spikes and camouflaged with sticks and branches. An unsuspecting solider could be badly injured and infected by the spikes, which were often purposely contaminated.

Violence had exploded in the United States as well. Prominent political figures during the 1960s—from President John F. Kennedy and Martin Luther King Jr. to Kennedy's brother Bobby—were assassinated. Homemade bombs and airplane hijackings added to the violence.

So a small group of researchers across the country, including those at the Southwest Research Institute, started to work together on detection projects. They wanted to know if dogs might help prevent such terrible crimes.

Dogs weren't the only potential detection species to interest the researchers. They added pigs to the mix. That wasn't much of a stretch. Since the fifteenth century the Italians and the French used pigs to find pricey truffles, a delicious fungus that attaches itself to tree roots.

If pigs find truffles beneath the soil, surely they could find buried land mines. The institute used red durocs, a handsome pig breed with drooping ears and marvelous large snouts.

The pigs, despite their intelligence and great olfactory systems, had drawbacks, said Jim Polonis, who managed many of the animal experiments in Texas.

First, the pigs were huge, up to four hundred pounds. And enthusiastic. They pulled on their leashes, dragging the handlers around. People found the idea of using pigs for law enforcement and the military laughable.

Even more difficult than their size was what pigs love to do: they love to root in the soil with those great snouts. Land mines easily explode.

So even though domestic pigs were smart and especially effective at sniffing out all sorts of materials, the Texas institute ultimately rejected them as sniffer animals.

That wasn't the end of animal experiments, though.

The researchers tried to train wild animals, birds of prey, and even snakes.

The experiments were failures. The deer couldn't search systematically. The rattlesnakes didn't bite the researchers, but instead of searching for scent, they liked

THE BEST BEAST OF ALL?

- Coyote
- Deer
- Javelina
- Raccoon
- Fox
- Badger
- Coati
- Timber wolf
- Civet cat
- Skunk
- Rattlesnake
- Hawk
- Pig

to doze in the Texas sun. Wolves and foxes were scared of people. The raccoons weren't awful when they were young, but as soon as they became adolescents, they started rebelling—and biting.

The behavioral scientists, project managers, and trainers at the Texas institute finally realized one important truth. Wild animals are wild.

Dogs don't have the most extraordinary noses in the animal kingdom. They can't slither into tiny holes like snakes, or leap over high fences as nimbly as deer.

But dogs are the right size for a number of tasks. They can heel at your side. They live long enough to make the training worthwhile. They aren't nocturnal (active at night) or diurnal (active during daylight) but are happy to be awake when their human companions are.

Above all, dogs want to partner with humans.

Like in the fairy tale "Goldilocks and the Three Bears," where Goldilocks tries out different beds and bowls of porridge, the researchers tried out different animals until they concluded that the dog was just right.

But it wasn't yet a fairy-tale ending. Dogs come in lots of shapes and sizes. Both the Texas institute and the military tried a number of dog breeds for different tasks and climates: Australian dingoes for hot climates, Norwegian elkhounds for cold. The scientists and project managers didn't experiment with mixes. That's because mutts can't be reproduced easily to get the same general dog from generation to generation.

While other breeds worked fine, the best all-around dogs for a multitude of tasks, the researchers found, were German shepherds and Labrador retrievers. They liked to hunt and to play. They were the right size. They had fine noses.

And no one would laugh at seeing one at a handler's side.

• • • • • • • • • •

Less than four months after I started training with Mike Baker, Solo and I took a test to certify as a cadaver-dog team.

It was a cold, blustery day in mid-November in the North Carolina foothills where I trained with the bloodhound handlers. Now I was taking a test alongside many of them. Several people who brought their dogs to certify decided not to test that day, given the wind and rain. I thought about coming back the next day, about spending another twenty-four hours in nervous anticipation.

But I grew up in Oregon. I tolerate rain. And Solo loves

Labrador retrievers and German shepherds were the top picks. Today more breeds, and even mixes, are used for scent detection.

rain. He doesn't think any weather is frightful as long as he can play in it.

The test materials had been set out earlier that day. It was soggy everywhere. The inside of the car was soaked, as I had kept the windows down for Solo. I was wet and cold. He was wet and smelly.

The hide inside the tobacco barn? No problem. Solo shoved the door open to get to it. The hide in the tree debris at the wood line was a cinch. And on it went.

The buried hide was the hardest. Solo didn't want to commit for what seemed like long minutes but was much less. He circled and sniffed while I stood away, at the edge of the field, arms crossed. When he finally lay down, he was right on top of it, I learned later from the testers.

He wasn't perfect. Solo acted like a know-it-all brat at the end of one find, not giving up his tug toy. I didn't know whether to smack him or to hug him since he had done so well. Neither was a good choice. Hugs are not his thing. Smacks are pointless.

I decided he deserved to tug a little longer. We couldn't get any wetter.

When I e-mailed Mike Baker that we had passed, he was his usual, practical self in his return e-mail.

"I just need your contact information. (The numbers you want us to use at three in the morning.)"

I'd never been so happy at the prospect of being startled awake by a phone ringing in the middle of the night.

It felt just right.

CHAPTER THIRTEEN

● ● ● ● ● ● ● ● ● ● ●

THE SWAMP

Police cars filled the parking lot. Radios crackled, and laptop screens glowed through tinted patrol car windows.

A few cops stood in a small group across the dismal lawn of the apartments. They looked up as my anonymous tan Camry slid toward them.

I lowered the rear window, and Solo stuck his huge head out. That was sufficient. One officer hitched his gun belt and jerked his head in a nod. Ten-four.

Then he gestured. They wanted me to drive over the curb and onto the patchy grass to be closer to where we would start the search.

This was not the first search that Solo and I had been

on that involved someone missing because of drug dealing. It was the first search with so many police and residents present.

I lowered the windows to give Solo plenty of air, got out of the car, and sorted through my minimal equipment in the trunk. The police were talking to the missing man's girlfriend. I heard her sobbing. More than one person was sobbing. They knew.

I leaned farther into the trunk to pull out my backpack, willing myself not to look. It wasn't my business. Making sure Solo and I did our best was my business.

The morning wind had calmed, and the late-spring air was heavy with unseasonable heat. The swamp would capture any scent that might be out there. It would be hanging like invisible moss on the vegetation, or floating above pools of water, waiting for Solo's nose to recognize it.

This was our first search where climate change probably played an indirect role. Three days before, a tempest of rain followed a drought, bringing flash floods. Sheets of water, silt, and trash slid off dry, hardened soil and pavement into huge storm drains, and all that water and muck dumped directly into the polluted wetlands and woodlands throughout the city.

This police case started with a 911 call several days before. The caller said that a group of men were selling drugs out of a car near the apartment complex. Police arrived and realized that one of the men was wanted for violating his parole.

When they went to arrest him, the suspect broke away and ran into the woods. One of the police K9s and his handler tried to track him. But it was dark, and by then the swamp was already flooded. The K9 nearly drowned trying to cross a swollen creek. The suspect was long gone, into the woods and the swamp beyond.

It was too dangerous to go back that night.

. . . .

The police called me when I was in the middle of a meeting in downtown Raleigh, twenty-seven miles away. I made an apologetic exit and dashed home. Solo watched and tried to trip me as I changed and grabbed my backpack, his water and toys, and a training aid.

Solo beat me to the car and waited impatiently for me to let him in.

Many areas inside Durham County
are swamps at least part of the year.

At the police station I left him in the car in the shade, windows down.

A room in the police station was already devoted to the search. I joined them and got brief introductions. Then police investigators and I stared at a large satellite map of the area. It was acres. Most of it would be muddy. Parts of it might still be flooded.

I tried for calm confidence, though my heart bounced around in my chest.

There in the station, we decided together how to run the search. I tried to sound as though I'd done this a lot, even while I confessed to the police standing around the table that I was a relative newbie.

Lots of cops were looking at me. I slowed down my voice, so I didn't sound like an eager amateur. I'm just a volunteer, I said. Dogs aren't perfect. They're just one tool among many.

I said all those things, and I believed them.

But when police call in a volunteer, they want results. I knew that as well. A couple dozen cops were on standby, expecting to search the area in a large sweep, flooded or not.

Unless Solo could find the missing man.

At least North Carolina woods and swamps were familiar ground to us. So when the police asked me what I needed, I asked for two people to come with us.

Even within city limits, a few acres of floodplain can contain sinkholes and creeks with sandy banks that can crumble beneath you. Two people could pull Solo or me out if either—or both—of us got stuck. What I didn't say was that I didn't want to be out there alone, in an area that might have dangerous people, as well as sinkholes.

I followed the unmarked car of two investigators who had cheerfully volunteered to accompany us to the apartment complex and beyond.

*   *   *   *   *   *   *   *   *   *   *

Once we all stood together on the dirt lawn, I realized that the two who volunteered to flank Solo and me were dressed for strolling down an office hallway, not slogging through a swamp. One wore nice tasseled loafers and creased tailored pants. His fellow investigator teased him about it, but he, too, wore office clothes that weren't designed as swamp gear.

The sharp dresser joked about water moccasins and copperheads, but he wasn't laughing that hard. I didn't tell him that water moccasins weren't very common in this part of North Carolina.

A couple of the bloodhound handlers I trained with told me that only people with phobias ever see venomous snakes. I like snakes, but I knew that wasn't true.

I looked like an Outward Bounder. I wore hiking boots with cross-country-skiing gaiters to discourage ticks that might carry diseases such as Rocky Mountain spotted fever or Lyme.

The heavy nylon gaiters also might deflect a copper-

Solo hated the harness, but sometimes
he had to wear it for his own safety.

head fang. Or not. No hat. I refused to look like a complete dork. I always used a fine-toothed flea comb after I was in the woods, to flick stray ticks out of my short hair.

As I let Solo out of the car, he provided sound effects — mewling, crooning, sounding more like a cheetah than a German shepherd. Even his whiskers twitched. I put on the sturdy nylon harness that he hated. It signaled constraint when he preferred freedom. Tough luck. I didn't need to attach the long line, as we would probably be far from roads, but his harness was staying on. It had a nice handle that I could use to suck him out of mudholes.

I ran down a final checklist in my head: water, water bowl, bug spray, an extra lead. Two rope toys. Thank goodness I hadn't forgotten those as I dashed out of the house. They were as essential as water.

With the permission of the commanding officer, a good distance away from the search area, I'd already planted a mason jar with dirt that had decomposition fluid in it. As sure as everybody seemed, we might not find anyone on the search. And Solo still needed to be rewarded.

Solo's paycheck.

My list-checking calmed me. Solo's distractions didn't calm him. He smelled dog pee on the jungle gym and dog pee on the Bermuda grass. His tail curled defensively.

As we walked toward the woods, children from the apartments—who stood back at first to watch from a distance—now surged around us. They leaped back and screamed in delighted fear as Solo swung his huge head in their direction. He wrinkled his brow. They weren't dogs. They were just small people. He relaxed his tail to wag, slow and low. Around children he dialed back both his drive and his noisiness.

"Don't worry. He's sweet," I told them. He wasn't always sweet with me, but he was with others. "He's big, huh? He won't hurt you. He loves kids." But Solo had a job to do, so we kept moving the whole time.

The two investigators, the dog, and I ducked under the yellow crime tape, climbed through a jagged hole in a chain-link fence, and entered the shade of the mimosas and elderberries and trees of heaven that overwhelmed the edges of these woods.

We straightened up on the other side, and I took one of the rope tug toys out of the training bag and then tucked it into my pocket. Solo yowled and spun, kneecapping me with his big shoulder. I winced and unhooked his lead. I reminded myself once again that searches were not the time for etiquette lessons. I didn't want Solo to sit or heel or watch me with adoration. I wanted him to find the suspect—who was now surely a victim.

Freed, and far more obedient off lead than on, Solo stood frozen, waiting. His eyes fixed forward, then sliced back to my pocket that held the tug toy, then shifted to

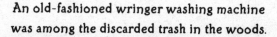

An old-fashioned wringer washing machine
was among the discarded trash in the woods.

Photo by Cat Warren

down the hill again. The slope was littered with empty liquor bottles, disposable diapers, a shattered Big Wheel, an ancient washing machine.

He didn't need to hear the command, but the words focused and centered me, reminding me that we'd rehearsed this game. The least I could do was get it started.

"Solo? Go find your Fish."

He did a final brief dance around me, striking the pocket where I'd stashed the toy with his open muzzle. Not a bite. It hurt, though. Then he barked sharply and disappeared into the dense undergrowth.

CHAPTER FOURTEEN

. . . .

A SERIOUS GAME

Solo bounded downhill, in that zigzaggy pattern that showed he was working. We left the grim apartments behind, and then the sound of police radios and children. We breached the first wave of Chinese privet. We avoided most but not all of the catbrier, which can dig its clawlike thorns through Solo's thick coat.

We were now in understory, filled with painted buckeye trees and small oaks. Hairy cords of poison ivy snaked around their trunks.

Then Solo took his first hot-dog leap, launching off a sandy cliff as it crumbled. He landed in the creek bed below. He was thrilled.

He distracted the two investigators, who had been

Solo ran hard through the understory.

Photo by D. L. Anderson

arguing about whether or not quicksand lay beneath the still-high water in the creek. They watched, slack-jawed, as Solo tested the two possibilities. He ran down the streambed and dropped his own jaw to scoop up water and sand. He humped his back like a porpoise, tucked his tail between his legs, spit out the sand, and then turned around and did it all over again. It wasn't quicksand.

I explained to the investigators that Solo was only momentarily being a show-off. Purpose and focus would arrive soon, I promised.

Solo could tell I was not amused. We were looking for a victim, not playing games.

Solo moved on. He put his nose down in the creek bed, then slowed to a crawl. He was working scent.

His tail set showed that he wasn't smelling an animal. That makes the kink defensive, held higher above his back. Nor was it his human-remains crick.

No, his tail showed he smelled scent left by a live

human. He surged out of the creek bed, right where a small portion of the cliff had collapsed on the far bank. The sedge grass there was bruised and broken.

I knew the police K9 hadn't made it that far. Neither had the police.

Deer, beaver, raccoon, and fox—the herbivores and midsize predators that manage to survive in these polluted woody swamps—don't create that much of a mess. It must have been a human. Or humans. It could have been the victim's family or friends.

Solo hasn't been trained or encouraged to do live trailing, except when I tell him to go find David in the house or yard. Solo's job is to hit the edge of cadaver scent and then range back and forth until he finds where it is most concentrated.

Ideally that spot would be the source. But in a swamp and woods of this size, it might be a long time before he hit scent. If he did.

It wasn't unreasonable to have Solo start his work from where the suspect most likely fled, the point last seen, or PLS. That was at the broken spot in the chain-link fence.

Solo didn't care where he started. He was playing his favorite game. The game, if he played well, that would end in his getting a rope tug toy.

But Solo had never found a body. Nor had he been exposed to an entire body during training. Solo was used to looking for smaller training aids. While he and I had worked on many acres at Nancy's farm, and I had watched him pick up scent from hides that were a couple hundred yards away, I had no idea what he might do in this case.

• • • • • • • • • • •

We continued to move downhill, past the creek, past the wood line. Now I could see the swamp. Except it didn't look like a swamp. It looked like a poison ivy nursery.

As far as I could see were thousands of immature plants, waist-high and neon green, with leaves the size of a toddler's hand. They waved at me in the slight breeze.

Here, in the open swamp, poison ivy plants don't have the opportunity to train themselves into hairy ropes that coil up trees. Poison ivy loves global warming. In the

Poison ivy is horrible for humans, but it helps many other species. This honeybee is gathering pollen from its flowers.

Photo by J. E. Spencer (CC)

Southeast it has been getting bigger, growing faster—and becoming more toxic.

I reminded myself that as much as I hate it, it's a native plant that feeds the locals. Songbirds—from the catbird to the Carolina wren—honeybees, deer, and muskrat benefit from its tiny blooms, leaves, and berries.

The baby plants grew together so closely that I knew I couldn't weave among those open palms without their touching me.

Solo demonstrated exactly how it shouldn't be done.

I barely saw him in the sea of green. He was more than a hundred feet away, creating a lively conga line of poison ivy, making them wave with even more enthusiasm. He plowed through, oblivious, harvesting their oils so they would transfer to me when I touched him.

Those plants also could hide a body. The suspect ran from the police at night in a downpour. He wouldn't have thought about poison ivy. The dark and rain would have hidden its identity in any case.

I didn't have much choice. I pulled down my long sleeves, buttoned them, raised my arms above the ivy, and followed Solo.

The two investigators followed us. It got swampier and swampier. Their shoes were getting soaked, but I heard no complaints.

We had cleared a section of the swamp when I suggested a temporary halt to cool Solo down.

He had quartered back and forth gamely, trying to

catch a whiff of human-remains scent. Nothing.

We'd been out for only twenty minutes or so, but it was eighty degrees. Solo, dashing around in his double-fur coat, was not quite hyperventilating, but close to it.

He was young and in great physical condition. But a scenting or tracking dog on the job tires more quickly than a dog out for a stroll. A scenting dog isn't just breathing but is deliberately pulling more air in, and then sending that air in a different direction once it's in his nose, in order to identify the scent. A sniffing dog breathes between one hundred forty and two hundred times a minute, compared with a dog out for an easy stroll, who breathes on average thirty times a minute.

Solo, being Solo, was running and sniffing.

We weren't lost, but we needed to figure out what area to search next. On the bright side, none of us had drowned or been injured. It was time to regroup. Solo found a patch of muddy swamp and flopped down, glassy-eyed, head flung up, dark lips pulled back to capture more oxygen. I poured him fresh water from my backpack.

Squinting in the bright sun, we humans eyed the map. We pointed to various landmarks on it, then found the corresponding creek beds and electrical towers around us. We figured out where the closest street was, which might be one direction the victim had fled. Or tried to.

Our conversation assumed a certain rationality on the part of the suspect. That wasn't a given. On the other hand, if he knew the area at all, it was likely that he'd moved toward where he thought the closest road was.

The water had receded greatly. I could see mud markings all around. Nonetheless, it was difficult to know exactly how high it had been that night.

I also realized that we should have started the search from the opposite side of the swamp. Solo might have been following a human trail at the beginning of the search, but there was a distinct possibility that we had been searching upwind for the victim.

We should have started downwind, on the other side of the swamp, to take advantage of the slight wind.

Soldiering on at this point was best. I picked up Solo's water bowl, flipped out the remaining ropes of saliva and water, and hitched the daypack onto my sweaty back.

• • • • • • • • • • •

Solo was happy to get back to work. He and I had trained for longer and longer searches. That training was now paying off with his willingness to wait for his reward.

It felt like years, but it was probably only five minutes later when I saw it. Solo slowed from his steady, quartering lope.

He lifted his head. He sampled the air. Then he threw his head higher, as if to gather in more news from the rafts of air.

We were now at the edge of the swamp and approaching a peninsula of trees and heavy brush. Solo angled toward it and slowed even more.

Solo hitting scent.

Then he lifted both front feet off the ground in a rearing motion. He looked like a small bear, swinging his head. He approached the edge of the trees.

His tail tensed into a tight curl, he moved closer and peered with suspicion up into the branches. I knew that curl. Solo was in cadaver scent. The heat of the day made the scent climb.

I suspected this particular victim was not in a tree, but I felt a flash of pride about Solo's looking upward. He was following scent. Dogs often search the ground obsessively, as though it is the source of all scent. But the world, and scent itself, is three-dimensional.

Despite my pride, I felt disoriented. This wasn't a training. The investigators were well behind us. I wasn't sure where. I'd been too intent watching Solo.

Solo followed his nose, and I followed Solo. We were

now deep into the shade of the trees on the far side of the swamp. As my eyes adjusted, I saw that he had stopped. He just stood there. About ten feet in front of him lay a body.

Facedown, shirtless, covered in mud. None of it felt real.

Solo looked back at me. What next?

I fumbled as I dragged his tug toy out of my pocket. I felt it catch and then give. I let my voice escalate. He'd done a good job.

"Good boy. Good boy. Good boy! What a good boy! Good Fish!"

Solo bounded over to get his reward, and I backed both of us away. Then he and I were swinging together, two planets spinning in a mud orbit, held together by the rope of a tug toy.

I pulled him farther and farther from the body trapped

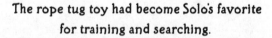

The rope tug toy had become Solo's favorite
for training and searching.

Photo by Nancy Hook

in the silt. I called over my shoulder, as loudly and matter-of-factly as I could, "Found him."

Over Solo's happy growls, I heard faint, surprised voices. They sounded far away, but one of them repeated himself, so I heard him more clearly as they ran toward us. "You're kidding. You're kidding. You're kidding."

Solo's work was done. He was tired. My heart pounded. I hitched him up, and we turned and walked toward the investigators, away from the canopy of trees. We were back in the sun and the bright green of the marsh.

I let him keep the tug toy. He had earned it.

CHAPTER FIFTEEN

. . . .

GRAINS OF SAND

These days, when I see more than three turkey vultures gliding in lazy circles in the thermals above me, I wonder if they are smelling something more than a dead animal below.

We keep track of the large birds of prey on searches. I've been called out on a missing-person case to search a particular area because a concerned citizen reported seeing eight or more vultures circling there.

They have such a keen sense of smell that it doesn't take much to attract them. One day I watched four vultures right next to our urban house competing over one squashed squirrel. They landed clumsily on our neighbor's roof before swooping down to squabble over a few ounces of rodent meat.

It's not just in the woods that my viewing habits have changed. I used to avoid television news, with its focus on violence and crime. Now I tune in on purpose if I know someone is missing. Especially if it's somewhere in North Carolina. Then I obsess about whether law enforcement might contact me. But unless they ask for volunteers to contact them, I don't call. It's not professional.

That doesn't keep me from wishing and hoping. I train Solo so he can search. He's a happy shadow who goes out in front of me.

The thinking I do about cases where we don't get called isn't entirely wasted. I learn from a distance. I use Google Maps to look at the area and terrain. If the general area of the missing person's point last seen has been covered in the news, I stare at the satellite view. I look at the dents in the vegetation and try to figure out if those dents represent a creek or a trail or a logging road.

Then I turn to my weather app. Knowing what wind and temperature and humidity have been in an area over several days matters—it's almost as important as knowing those things while you are searching. With the right conditions, scent can get caught in places and stay there.

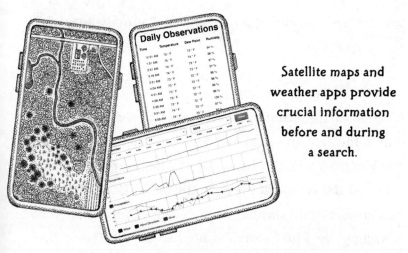

Satellite maps and
weather apps provide
crucial information
before and during
a search.

A cadaver-dog handler also needs to know what bodies look like after a few days, or weeks, or months out in their specific environment. Bodies are rarely pretty in early stages of decomposition, but within a couple of weeks, they can fade into their environment like chameleons.

Some of my friends and acquaintances make mournful faces and comment that it must be rewarding but certainly not enjoyable work.

For me it's both, even with the sadness and the tension. I train Solo and myself because, first and foremost, it is fun. You shouldn't do something that makes you unhappy all the time. And an unhappy dog won't work at all.

I don't dread getting called out. I hope we are. It's a challenging puzzle that pushes me and Solo to our mental and physical limits.

Plus, I get outside, often in the woods. I can watch Solo

use his nose. That, for me, is one of the most beautiful sights on earth.

• • • • • • • • • • •

It's fun to train, but it's never easy to search. On one search the detective flanking me asked whether a cadaver dog can miss a body. I looked at the dense woods on one side and the clear-cut mess on the other. Logs there lay crisscrossed, with shrubby growth coming up in between. A swamp we'd just searched lay behind us. Recent tire tracks were visible along the dirt road.

We were now working back along a logging road, punching into the woods in several places where old deer

North Carolina woods can be thorny and dense, filled with undergrowth and hidden fences.

Pixabay

trails, or even a break in the vines and briars, provided an entry. Our working theory was that if we couldn't get through it, someone trying to carry a body wouldn't have an easy time either.

If Solo hits scent, he follows it. But an exhausted, panting dog isn't great at scenting. Plus, Solo's nose has to be in the proper place. Hasty searches over dozens of acres filled with brush and trees don't give 100 percent coverage. Several dogs are ideal.

Everyone does their best—a bit of whacking with a machete when it's feasible, saving energy when you can see a spot for entry just ahead.

So when the detective asked me if a dog can miss a body, I had to nod. Yes.

I think about it all the time.

There are three options on searches. Two of them I can live with. The third option gives me nightmares.

The first option is as close to ideal as you can get, given that you are looking for someone who is most likely dead. You and the dog play a role—any role—on a search, and the person is found. It doesn't matter if someone else, or someone else's dog, finds the body. That person's disappearance and death is usually sad, sometimes tragic. But finding that person is important. A good example is when we found the man in the swamp. It didn't give me nightmares. It represented a success. Solo did good work.

Option two is not finding the missing person because

they aren't in the area being searched. Most searches end with no victim found, but it's still important to search those areas. Because the area is, for instance, the woods behind the house of an elderly man who wandered away. Or it's a spot where known drug addicts, including the victim, go to buy their drugs.

Option two haunts me more than option one. My mind keeps poking at the possibilities, wondering about the weaknesses in the overall search strategy, in the dog's work, in my work. Option two involves trying to imagine what happened at the end for that victim, and where, and how. It can stretch out for years. Or longer.

Nonetheless, it too falls within the realm of normal. Missing people sometimes stay that way. In the United States the list of "endangered" people, who are probably dead, had nearly forty-six thousand entries in 2017.

But the nightmare of not finding someone belongs to the missing person's family and friends, not to me.

My nightmares about searches—the nightmares that rightfully belong to me—arise from option three: if I ever find out that we missed someone or something in an area we were responsible for searching. I know a number of handlers who feel the same way. It's a unique dread. As much as I hate an occasional false alert—when the dog says something is there and it's not—I hate a false negative even more. That's when a dog ignores or accidentally overruns scent that's out there, or you don't properly cover the area you were assigned.

Solo is almost always happy, and that can help make difficult searches a little easier.

Photo by Juli Leonard

It can happen.

This is the reality of searching: the missing person you are looking for is so infinitely small, so lost in the wide world, that they might never be found.

And yet it isn't all mournful. Toward the end of a day of hard searching on another case, two investigators and I watched Solo. We had a final, low-probability area we needed to clear. Solo should have been exhausted. Instead he levitated like a black-and-red kangaroo through the high grass, backlit by an early evening sunset. Despite the sadness of the case, he made us smile.

I drove home so tired that night that even the tickle

of a tick on my neck elicited only a flick from my finger. Solo, dried mud flaking off his guard hairs, was sacked out on the backseat. He didn't have a whine left in him.

• • • • • • • • • • • • •

Before I tackle a new kind of search, I go back and hit the research.

Take a person with dementia. Their behavior differs from that of other lost people. If an unimpaired person is right-handed and gets lost in the woods, they'll tend to move to the right.

Not someone with dementia. That person doesn't behave logically, even subconsciously. They'll walk straight into thick blackberries. Their brain can't compute turning around or backing up. They will keep walking in place until they drop.

The body of a man with Alzheimer's was found in the woods two streets away from his suburban home, a month after he went missing. The police, I heard through the grapevine, had been given my name and number soon after he went missing. The call never came. There could be a hundred good reasons why they never reached out. Or none.

It was one of those times when I sat and waited for a call that didn't come.

Most people with dementia or Alzheimer's—nearly 90 percent—are found less than a mile from their point of departure and within thirty yards of a road. I know that because when I was waiting for the call, I studied the case.

It wasn't wasted effort. I used that knowledge for other searches.

But I still think about that one man and his family. Perhaps even more than if I had been called out.

I go back to the books every time. First to the *Cadaver Dog Handbook* and then further afield.

How do you deploy your dog properly along a road-side? How many yards back might a panicked or lazy murderer drag a victim? Not far. Twenty-five yards. Check farther back.

Animals are more industrious than most humans. They need to feed themselves and their families. How far might they drag something? It depends on the animal.

Then there are the obvious easy areas that need searching: abandoned properties and outbuildings; piles of wood and debris that can be used to conceal a body; illegal garbage dumps, where someone can drag an old mattress over the body.

For "clandestine" or secretive burials, murderers often take advantage of existing natural holes made by roots and erosion. They don't have to dig as long.

Did the suspect have easy access to a shovel? Wasn't he homeless? Most clandestine burials are no deeper than two and a half feet, yet that's enough for someone to dis-appear forever.

There's also the time frame to consider. In North Carolina, areas can get overgrown in one season.

Hunters tend to find skeletal remains more often than law enforcement officers do. Mostly skulls, as they are the easiest to identify. A turkey hunter found a skull more than a year and a half after a victim disappeared.

Other bones tend to blend in with leaf litter. But anyone who has searched in North Carolina woods knows that heart-stopping moment when you see a light-brown or green-moss-covered turtle shell, a hump coming out of the surrounding humus, and momentarily mistake it for a skull.

On one case police jokingly—but with an underlying awareness of the neighborhood surrounding the woods—asked me to please find only the body they were looking for. On another case, searchers found skeletal remains, but not the victim.

Searching sounds scary. But it's not. For all the cruel casualness of people and of nature, there's something reassuring about working with a good cadaver dog.

Finding someone's remains can give closure to a family or allow the police or prosecutors to move ahead with a case. That doesn't entirely explain why it's so important.

It's partly to be able to acknowledge, even momentarily, the spot where someone rested. And to think on it. I like the fact that, animal predation aside, it can be hard to get rid of a body.

When people die, they don't completely disappear. Yes, they cease to exist. At the same time, they also stubbornly stick around.

During one search, Solo went right to a spot in the woods, lay down, and looked at me expectantly. An investigator confirmed that on that spot, more than a year earlier, hunters had found the bones of a murder victim. The pine forest floor held on to her scent and would do so for years.

Solo lay in the woods and looked at me. He wanted his reward.

CHAPTER SIXTEEN

. . . .

MOUSE JUICE

Roy Ferguson arrived at the cadaver-dog training in Georgia decked out in a fluorescent orange sweatshirt and a tan vest covered with flaps and pockets, gadgets and badges.

He looked like an ideal Scout troop leader: geeky, capable of goofy humor, yet stern enough to keep mischief at bay.

On this particular misty winter morning, his voice was somber and curt. That's because while he was pretending to be a homicide detective, the purpose was serious.

Good trainers create complicated practice sessions that help prepare handlers and dogs for real searches.

Roy Ferguson is a fine actor and a search expert.

There's a saying that fits nicely: "Train hard, search easy."

Everyone was going to train hard that day.

I'd driven down to Georgia without Solo the day before. It was a four-hundred-mile trip, but I wanted to learn from the best. I also wanted to take notes and photographs and not worry about Solo stuck in the car, bored and frustrated, while I watched other dogs and interviewed people.

I needed training and instruction as much as he did— if not more. It was much easier to concentrate without a demanding dog at my side. I wanted to be a composed student, not a nervous handler.

When I arrived at the large cabin I'd be staying at, I knew I'd made the right choice. Lounging people— with their border collies, golden retrievers, and German shepherds—looked up when I opened the door. The people smiled. The dogs wagged their tails gently.

I slept soundly for the most part, and was awoken only here and there by a startled bark or growl. That was a given, with seven or eight dogs and their people crowded into an unfamiliar cabin. I lulled myself back to sleep with the pleasant thought that those growls weren't from Solo.

The next morning, fully awake, I stood next to Roy as he briefed a dog handler from Florida. Roy held a clipboard filled with mysterious sheets of information. I held a small reporter's notebook, with a large camera strapped around my neck.

Ben Ortiz and June Bug, Ben's young American pit bull terrier, stood in front of Roy. June Bug's sheriff K9 vest provided the only bulk on her slender brindle body.

We were seventy-five yards down a gravel logging road in Georgia that wound into the woods and disappeared. It was the kind of road that someone might drive down at night when he's panicked, looking for a place away from headlights and homes, to dispose of a body.

An eighteen-month-old toddler was missing, Roy

told Ben. That was fake. He went on. Law enforcement had discovered a possible grave site down the trail behind them.

That was fake too, but the dog wouldn't know that. If Roy had buried human remains there for the training, it was good practice for an actual burial.

And Roy's stern and somber voice made everything seem real.

"Work your dog in the area, come out, and tell me what you've found."

Ben nodded and released June Bug. She bounced down the trail like a small gazelle, beelined to a mound of freshly dug earth, sniffed long and carefully, went to another mound farther back in the woods, cut her ghostly amber eyes at Ben, and snatched something off the mound.

"Get back to work," Ben said softly. Still munching, June Bug skittered sideways and leaped over a log.

Sometimes you need your meals to go.

Whatever the crunchy delight was, it gave her what she needed to settle down. She moved away, and so did Ben. She quartered back and forth. I followed at a distance.

Five minutes later, though it seemed longer, Ben reported back to Roy. Nothing, he told Roy. No alerts. Both men's faces were blank.

Roy thanked Ben. Ben nodded, shrugged, snapped on June Bug's leash, and led her back to his SUV. Her whip-thin tail was tucked between her legs.

Roy kept his face expressionless until the two

June Bug, an American pit bull terrier, at a Georgia training.

disappeared down the trail. Then he smiled. "I like the way that dog works."

He also meant he liked the way Ben worked June Bug on this fake-burial-within-a-fake-burial scenario. Ben didn't try to convince his dog that human remains were there when they weren't. And June Bug was honest— except for that minor moment of treat snatching.

But Ben, like the other handlers, had to wait until the end of the day to hear how he and June Bug had done. This too is similar to real searches. You clip up your dog, shake the investigator's hand, and walk away. Sometimes you never learn if police find something.

Roy isn't a homicide detective. He's an optician from a small town in Tennessee. He and his wife, Suzie—who also looks like an ideal Scout leader but is an office manager—were training handlers in Eatonton, Georgia.

The burial problem was only the first in a long day of Suzie and Roy toying with handlers' minds and challenging their dogs. To start the morning with an elaborate scenario where there's no training material for the dogs to find may seem cruel.

Training, though, needs to simulate reality. Mostly, on actual searches you don't find what you're looking for. On most trainings you do.

In the missing-toddler case, it was worse. A number of handlers had driven or flown hundreds of miles to attend the seminar. And the first training on the first day? No training aids put out.

Most of the handlers that morning, anticipating that cadaver-training material must be planted *somewhere*, talked first themselves and then their dogs into thinking that a freshly dug mound had to be a grave. A number of dogs alerted there, partly because the handlers expected something to be there.

One doesn't need to invent training scenarios. Cases themselves provide the best material. Roy and Suzie's mentor, Art Wolff, a detective and K9 trainer, developed the practice sessions I saw that day. The toddler case was adapted from a 2007 case. Police found what looked like a fresh grave and called Roy and Suzie's team. Roy

Dogs love hoof clippings that come from
a farrier trimming horses' feet.

went to the scene with his German shepherd, Cherokee.

Cherokee ignored the grave.

Police dug anyway. It *was* a grave—but for a dead pit bull.

Setting up realistic trainings is crucial for successful searches. It's not only handlers who get into trouble. Dogs, if they aren't conditioned to search for a long time without a reward, can want to find something a little too much.

False alerts, where the dog thinks something is there and it's not, can have bad consequences—fruitless days of digging for law enforcement, or charges against someone that prove false.

After watching a few dogs work, I realized that Roy and Suzie had made the case extra hard. They scattered smelly horse hoof clippings on top of one "grave" to entice the dogs and irritate the handlers. Something like that is called a "distraction" in detection training. That was what June Bug had grabbed for her to-go meal.

Still, June Bug and Ben did better on this problem than most of the other teams. Other dogs grabbed the hoof clippings too, and their handlers got increasingly stuck, staring at the graves as their dogs hesitated and sniffed the tempting piles of dirt.

It got worse. Several dogs alerted on the second fake grave.

Earlier that morning Roy had poured a generous shot of mouse juice across the top.

Mouse juice was Roy and Suzie's invention. They discovered it by accident on a cross-country drive. They had some frozen mice in a bag in an ice chest that they were already planning to use as a training distraction.

It got hot in their SUV. The ice melted, the bag broke, the dead mice swam free.

"Holy cats!" Suzie said, her eyes wide with the memory of opening the chest. The smell must have been staggering.

"Cool!" Roy said.

He had a hypothesis: the liquid was smellier than

the original dead mice. Roy poured it onto a mound of dirt. Dozens of blowflies arrived within seconds. Hypothesis probably correct. Mouse juice became an essential element in Roy and Suzie's training.

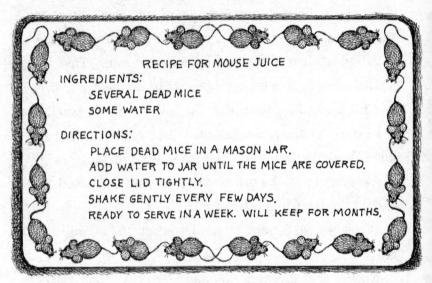

RECIPE FOR MOUSE JUICE

INGREDIENTS:
SEVERAL DEAD MICE
SOME WATER

DIRECTIONS:
PLACE DEAD MICE IN A MASON JAR.
ADD WATER TO JAR UNTIL THE MICE ARE COVERED.
CLOSE LID TIGHTLY.
SHAKE GENTLY EVERY FEW DAYS.
READY TO SERVE IN A WEEK. WILL KEEP FOR MONTHS.

Suzie and Roy don't do this simply to annoy the handlers or to tease the dogs. Dead animals can be everywhere on a search. Dogs need to learn to ignore them.

In the late afternoon debriefing, Roy explained to a group of chagrined handlers what had happened.

A slightly buried animal carcass, he pointed out, is even better for training dogs. "Roadkill is phenomenal!" Roy declared, beaming.

During the debriefing several handlers explained why their dogs had failed, and why it wasn't either their or their dogs' fault.

Roy and Suzie listened carefully, nodded sympathetically, and then gently told those handlers not to make excuses for poor performance. Even if the dogs were getting bully sticks or cow hooves as a bedtime treat, they shouldn't snack on the job.

The hoof-and-mouse humiliation was just the first challenge of the day.

• • • • • • • • • • • •

Before the winter sun set in Georgia, Roy and Suzie played with the minds of numerous handlers in numerous ways. In another scenario, they instructed the handlers to search only within a yellow-crime-taped area. But they had set up the training so that the wind was bringing the scent of human remains from where Roy and Suzie had planted the training material, under a creek bank—well outside of the yellow-taped confines.

Roy tried to tip off the handlers before the search. He said there were bears in the area. Bears are good at carting their food around. Everyone has to eat. Cadaver-dog handlers need to know if bears inhabit the area they are searching.

The dogs kept throwing their heads wistfully toward the scent. Their handlers kept calling them back.

"She's pulled him off three times," Roy muttered as he watched one handler urge her dog to come back and search within the limits of the tape as Roy, playing the role of a local sheriff, had directed them. The dog sulkily obeyed her.

But one handsome golden retriever, called back several times, did the right thing and ran away, ignoring his
handler's pleas. All I could see was his tail, wagging furi-
ously underneath a mountain laurel that tumbled over
the creek bank. The handler meekly asked Roy—standing
by, clipboard in hand—for permission to search that area.

Roy nodded and tried not to show his relief. The dog
had found the garbage bag containing human-remains
training material. What a good dog!

That disobedient golden acted just like Suzie's dog,
Schatzie, and a teammate's dog during a search in
Tennessee. When Suzie's team had been called to try to
recover remains from a double homicide involving the
Russian mob, law enforcement asked handlers to search
one area. Instead the dogs were interested in going where
the scent was.

The two dogs' unwillingness to stay within the confines of the search area helped the police recover human
remains from an undercut creek bed.

"When your canine shows interest, you really have to
trust your dog. You really do," Roy told the handlers later
that day. "You've got to follow your dog. Your dog is out
there trying to do a job. You say, 'Excuse me, is there any
reason I can't search this?'"

Then he switched roles from bad cop to good cop
because Roy is a sweet person and can play bad cop for
only so long. "That's a difficult case to work," he admitted.

The scenarios that Roy and Suzie presented that day in

Georgia highlight how hard it is to fight human nature. If there are thick briars, or steep rocky slopes, or stern officials who have set unrealistic boundaries, it can be difficult.

It's one reason you want to bring in good stubborn dogs. They're willing to ignore you and go into hard-to-get-at places. They don't think about crime tape or worry about poison ivy. They're following their noses.

Suzie Ferguson gives her cadaver dog,
Schatzie, a drink before working.

CHAPTER SEVENTEEN

. . . .

THE ZOMBIE HANDLER

T rust your dog."

Handlers say this all the time. Sometimes they wear T-shirts with that saying emblazoned on them, so that they can glance down and be reminded.

But with every saying there's an opposite saying. For me that phrase is "Don't be stupid."

Dogs have brains with lots of space dedicated to scent. People have brains that have lots of space dedicated to being able to read a Marvel comic book, or write a sonnet, or design a better escalator.

I trusted Solo, but I had a problem. I was starting to idolize him. He had helped find missing people. He was more than five years old, smart, cheerful, fearless, independent. He was now able to ignore other dogs when he worked.

Mostly, Solo was becoming likable. He smiled constantly, his mouth open and relaxed, big teeth gleaming. He went into high drive during training and searches but relaxed with David and me at home. He was my partner and our companion.

After one long, difficult search, I said something to David I regret. I was tired. I shouldn't have said it, but at that moment I meant it. "He's my hero."

Solo's success had made me doe-eyed and brainless. I was in danger of becoming a zombie handler.

I looked around at seminars and trainings. I wasn't alone. Handlers stood by passively, sometimes watching their own dogs work. And instead of observing and learning while others worked their dogs, they chatted idly or paid little attention. They had been made brainless by the fantasy that their dogs were perfect—and could solve complex puzzles by themselves.

Dogs do some things much better than humans. Other things? Not so well. They're much better at scent work than we are, but we don't hand them the car keys and tell them to show up at a

Solo's good nose sucked some of my brains out.

search and then report back what they've found.

Handlers need to set their dogs up for success. That means partnering with your dog. Dogs need to be put in the right spot to do their job. That means more than starting your dog downwind of where you think the victim or training material might be. Sometimes, depending on how old the remains are, it's better to start them upwind.

I needed to learn when to step aside and let Solo do what he does best, and when to guide him. I needed to keep my eyes and mind open, and think about all the variables that might affect scent: weather over several days, wind eddies, how long the victim had been lost, what police knew or didn't know about the case. What they might have gotten wrong.

It's not a dog's job to know all that.

Nancy Hook snapped at me one day when I was wandering aimlessly in a large field. "You call that a pattern?"

I was stumbling along, lazily waiting for Solo to read my mind and figure out where I wanted him to search.

● ● ● ● ● ● ● ● ● ● ●

Months after watching Roy and Suzie train in Georgia, I had yet another chance to realize how much I had to learn. I was in Mississippi. It was early fall, and the cypress trees, their roots dug deep in the water and their knees exposed, were turning gold and crimson. Monarch butterflies fluttered by, migrating south before the first frosts.

Lisa Higgins of Pearl River, Louisiana, is one of the many

handlers who has trained with Andy Rebmann and gone on to become a top cadaver-dog handler and trainer herself.

If L. Frank Baum, the author of *The Wonderful Wizard of Oz*, had spent his life in Louisiana, the Good Witch of the South might have looked like Lisa Higgins. She has large hazel eyes slanting at the corners, a strong nose, round cheeks with slight freckles, and short salt-and-pepper springy hair. Her voice is soft, precise—and firm when needed.

When she laughs, which is often, it's a merry peal.

Lisa has responded to many hundreds of searches

Lisa Higgins is an experienced handler and trainer who, while serious, is humorous and kind.

Photo by Cat Warren

across the United States and Canada since she started training her first cadaver dog, a golden retriever, in 1990. On Frosty's first official search, in 1991, she helped pinpoint the victim's location, under four feet of water and three feet of sand.

Over the past two decades, Lisa has also worked with the FBI on numerous cases.

Now she has Dixee, a wild Malinois–German shepherd cross, and Maggie, an aging Australian shepherd who looks like a well-loved stuffed panda.

Lisa knows a lot, not just about dogs and wind and scent but also about human behavior, both good and bad. Because knowing what people might do can help handlers help their dogs—whether it's finding a patient who wandered away from a nursing home or finding the victim of a homicide.

Lisa had set up "a little problem" in Mississippi for handlers—a simple scenario with some shallowly buried training material.

The handlers weren't just to release their dogs to look for scent. Instead Lisa asked them to focus their search using something called the Winthrop Point.

No one in the group had heard of the Winthrop Point. I hadn't. I doubt that anyone forgot after Lisa described it.

The Winthrop Point was named after an investigator who realized that he saw a grim pattern emerge in clandestine burials.

Killers were doing the same thing that soldiers used

to do when they needed to bury excess weaponry so that the enemy wouldn't get access to it. The military needed to know how to get back to the guns or grenades they had buried.

Murderers sometimes want to return to visit the secret site where they buried their victims, but they also want to know if law enforcement is getting close.

The Winthrop Point, Lisa explained, is a distinctive landmark that won't burn, rot, or change. That means trees can't be a Winthrop Point because they can fall down. Gravel roads are out. Roads can come and go. A huge boulder might work. A large concrete sewer drain. Some permanent fixture in the landscape.

Lisa asked each handler to look around in the growing darkness and try to find a nearby point that might serve as a Winthrop Point.

She was standing in a large state park, about ten yards from a large metal contraption with chains, its pole buried deep in concrete. It was a disc golf basket. Distinct. Unmovable. Oddly permanent.

Yet only one or two handlers saw it. It seemed like such an innocent object—like a maypole with chains. They are a common sight in large parks that have elevation changes, creeks, and trees.

Lisa pointed it out to the puzzled handlers and then oriented them more. They needed to think like a killer. Downhill, the trees were too open for someone to feel comfortable getting rid of a body.

A target for disc golf, which is often played in large parks.

Uphill, though, was wooded, hidden, private. That was where handlers should start their dogs searching.

How far back should they send their dogs?

Lisa informed handlers that the vast majority of body disposals are less than a hundred feet from a road. This is something handlers need to know to give their dogs the best chance of success.

Once the handlers were properly oriented off the Winthrop Point, they could in turn orient their dogs. If they were zombie handlers before, they weren't now.

The next day it was Lisa's eleven-year-old grand-daughter's turn to work her dog. Haylee Carney had just started to train Jayda, a year-old female sable shepherd with manic energy.

Haylee has an angelic, somber face and soft brown curls. She says "yes, ma'am" and "no, ma'am," especially to her "MaMa," Lisa, who helps homeschool her. It was time for some away-from-home schooling.

"Haylee, you've been listening," Lisa said. "What's the Winthrop Point?"

Haylee rattled off the answer. "Where somebody puts a body where he can find it again. He uses a landmark."

"Why does he do it, Haylee?"

"So he knows when law enforcement is getting close."

"And what else?"

Haylee didn't have an immediate answer, so Lisa

Haylee had just started training and handling her young German shepherd, Jayda.

Photo by Cat Warren

gently reminded her. "So he can visit the body whenever he wants. Why?"

Lisa knew the answer might be hard for Haylee to understand. So Lisa answered her own question with precision. "Because he's a sick little puppy, that's why."

Haylee nodded, unafraid. "Yes, ma'am."

Then Haylee ran her dog.

• • • • • • • • • • • •

When I saw Haylee again, more than a month later, she and her MaMa were in another state. Lisa was training more handlers. Brad Dennis, who searches for missing children across the nation, was there as a trainer too. Brad can be funny when it helps and serious when he needs to be.

Haylee was sitting and learning, taking notes, this time at an evening seminar Brad was teaching. He was instructing handlers on searching for abducted children and teenagers. Brad, like Lisa, knows about the worst but manages to find and bring out the best in people.

Along with Haylee and her grandmother, the room that night was filled with tired volunteer and law enforcement handlers. They had worked their dogs most of the day. I had worked Solo, who was finally sleeping in the car. Haylee had worked Jayda.

A few people took notes, but most didn't. They were sprawled, exhausted. Haylee was an exception. She was bent over her notebook, writing madly. Homeschooling never ends.

Brad Dennis, who helps organize searches across the nation, works a river training with Chance, a cadaver dog.

Brad gave the group a scenario from a case that he worked on. It ended, as many do, tragically. In every abduction case, hours, even minutes, count.

A seventeen-year-old disappears while jogging. What should different agencies do? Get tracking dogs on the ground immediately. Know exactly where to deploy them. Know how to organize people around the immediate area of interest. Know the area. Look for trails. Figure out quickly where to look first. Take well-meaning but inexperienced volunteers and send them to the outer edges of the search area so that experienced searchers and dogs can concentrate on the high-probability areas.

Brad noted, with sadness, that even with the effort, it was too late for this particular victim.

Haylee's hand shot up. She was polite but unapologetic. "Could you go back to the last slide, please?" she asked Brad. Her head was still hunched over her notes. She hadn't gotten down every single detail of what the standard victim of abduction looks like.

People shifted in their chairs uneasily. They were a little horrified. This was adult business. And the standard victim can look a lot like Haylee.

But Brad, like Lisa, is a firm believer in teaching young people what to look for and think about. He clicked back to the previous PowerPoint slide. Haylee thanked him.

Brad continued with his lecture. He talked about "the freeze moment." He showed a grainy bank security video. The girl in the video turned and stood stock-still as her killer approached. That hesitation was all it took; she was gone.

All of us, Brad said, have this "awesome, God-given gift." That moment when the hair stands up on the back of your neck. "As soon as you feel that? Use it."

Now all the major organizations dealing with abduction have changed their tune on what potential young victims should do, he said.

Brad looked at the class to see if we knew what the new advice of abduction experts was.

Haylee's hand shot up again. All of us were focused, no longer tired.

MaMa, she said, had told her what to do. "If you let them take you someplace else, they will hurt you twice as bad, so you better bite, scratch, kick, and take all the DNA you can."

THE LOWDOWN ON DNA

Haylee is right. DNA evidence can play an important role in solving a crime. All it takes is a few cells to get enough DNA information to identify a suspect. Scraped-off skin cells can be an ideal way to link a suspect to a crime. DNA evidence can be valuable in criminal investigations because it's almost impossible for someone to have DNA that is identical to another person's. Scientists have discovered that even identical twins don't have identical DNA!

But DNA is delicate and can be easily contaminated or damaged. Heat, sunlight, time, or even breathing on or touching a sample can make that sample useless. So it's important for forensic investigators to use caution when they gather samples—and not introduce their own DNA onto a piece of evidence.

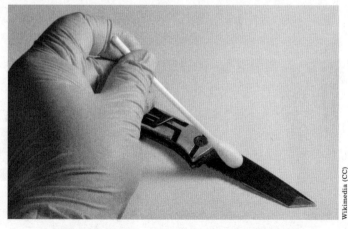

Wikimedia (CC)

A forensic scientist uses a cotton swab to gather DNA evidence from a knife

Lisa beamed. Brad nodded. The handlers clapped.

Haylee is unafraid. She's smart and studious, curious about the world and all it holds, both the bad and the good.

· · · · · · · · · · · ·

Seven months later I saw Haylee at another event. She appeared to have grown several inches. She had news for me. Immature, energetic Jayda, working in tandem with more experienced dogs, helped pinpoint a drowning victim.

Haylee is a cadaver-dog handler in training. Even with her MaMa, and the great education she and her dog are receiving, she will make mistakes. Everyone does.

I doubt that she'll go through a zombie-handler phase.

And if she does, it will be brief.

CHAPTER EIGHTEEN

· · · · · · · · ·

DOG TALES AND HORSE HOOEY

Here's another thing people say a lot: "Dogs don't lie." Nonsense. Dogs can be great at lying.

They lie in the kitchen, for instance, eyeing you a full hour before dinner. I'm starving. I think you forgot to feed me this morning. See these ribs? See this drool?

They lie in the living room, staring at the dark gap under the sofa where their ball has rolled. Then they turn their large brown eyes to you. I can't possibly get to that toy. Help, please?

Of course they could get it. But it's easier to train you to squeeze your arm under the couch to retrieve the ball covered with dust bunnies.

Solo isn't that different. He's got a fine nose. He's

clever and devoted. Mike Baker says that Solo is one of the most honest dogs he knows.

Solo is also capable of lying.

It's rare, but Solo is happy to skip a step in training if it leads to a good outcome—a game of tug. If he's not entirely sure about the placement of a hide, or if it's a new training sample that he hasn't encountered before, or if he's worked long and hard and gotten frustrated? He might take an educated guess rather than do the hard work of pinpointing it.

But for cadaver training, close isn't good enough—especially if I know that he can get closer. In actual searches, not getting close enough can mean the difference between recovering evidence or missing it entirely. And during searches, precision often falls off a bit because

Photo by D. L. Anderson

I know it's pretty close. It's somewhere around here!
Isn't this good enough?

you, the dog, and law enforcement are working with lots of unknowns.

An important part of my job as Solo's handler is to prevent him from getting sloppy. I don't always perform perfectly.

Here's just one example: We were in an abandoned warehouse in Durham. A K9 handler had obligingly put out some training hides for Solo. They had "cooked," as one says about all sorts of scent-training material (not just cadaver), for about a half hour.

The warmer the air, the more quickly cadaver-training aids can send out scent for Solo to find. I expect they weren't being stingy and holding back scent that hot night.

Solo pulled hard to get into the building. The handler who put out the hides followed us. After I released Solo, he hurtled through the building, accelerating madly, trying to dig his claws into the concrete for extra momentum.

His head twisted. He flipped, flew back to a garbage can, and came in for a slow, deep sniff.

It was so pretty. I caught up with him and stopped, admiring his fine technique.

Solo eyed me as I stood there, stupidly meeting his gaze.

He then crouched gradually into his final alert, continuing to stare at me. Something felt wrong—like he was acting, rather than reacting to scent.

I looked back at the other handler, who hadn't paid

close attention, and who gave me a head shake. Nope. No cadaver hide there.

Certainly something smelly lurked in the garbage can. Maybe a piece of Kentucky Fried Chicken?

My bad timing, when I slowed down and stared at Solo, helped trigger what's called a false alert. I unconsciously encouraged him to do what he shouldn't have done.

Solo's behavior might become a bad habit if I didn't sharpen my game. I made a sloppy beginner's error that night. The mistake I avoided? Rewarding him with his tug toy.

I broke off my gaze and repeated the command: "Go find your Fish."

My voice probably had an edge, although it shouldn't have. Solo moved on to find the hides the K9 handler had put out for him.

"That's why we call it training," Mike Baker said in a neutral tone after I had put Solo in the car.

Mike was irked that the other handler hadn't stopped Solo and me before we started our do-si-do around the can.

He was rightfully irritated with me.

I was mad at me.

• • • • • • • • • • •

False alerts aren't Solo's fault. They're mine. But I inherited the problem from our earliest ancestors. We humans, accidentally and on purpose, encouraged dogs to be responsive to us. That started many thousands of years ago, when wolves and humans were deciding whether they wanted to hang out together.

One theory about how wolves were domesticated is that bolder wolves got more food and human waste. Their love of our garbage led them closer and closer to us. Once we had squirming wolf cubs in our laps, we were toast. Another, less likely, theory is more romantic. Humans found that wolves helped us hunt.

We generally say that humans are the ones who did the choosing. We chose certain wolves who became wolf-dogs who became dogs. A few evolutionary biologists have another take. We coevolved. Wolves may have chosen us and changed us too. And perhaps wolf-dogs, if they helped humans hunt and kept an eye out for intruders, freed humans to develop and evolve in other ways?

Perhaps a bold, curious ancestor of this modern wolf
helped create the dog.

CUSTOM-MADE FOR CONSUMPTION

Plants and pollinators—species that help the plants reproduce—have worked out a sweet deal. Bees, wasps, flies, and birds help plants and flowers reproduce, and get a nectar meal in return. Their relationship is the result of millions of years of coevolution, where each species influences the other's evolution.

Many trumpet-shaped flowers likely coevolved with pollinators such as hummingbirds.

• The flowers' bright (usually red) colors attract the hummingbird. Bees can't see red, and it's a hummingbird's favorite color!

• The hummingbird's bill fits easily into these flowers, thanks to the flowers' long, narrow shape.

• The flowers evolved to bloom during hummingbirds' breeding season, when the birds need sugary snacks the most.

Photo by Charles J. Sharp (CC)

A purple-throated carib gets a nectar meal from a flower.

Mutual affection. This gaze helps with bonding.

Today? The majority of domestic dogs want to please us—or at least, not avoid us. They need and love food and shelter, and that helps them love us. In turn we love their companionship, their wagging tails, their adoring eyes. That mutual gaze fires off a feel-good chemical called oxytocin in both human and dog brains.

The advantages of dogs wanting to please us are obvious. It can help humans and dogs work as a team. In the house and even during obedience exercises, it's wonderful to have a dog who stares lovingly at you. A dog can follow your gaze or pointed finger to see what you're looking at.

Like a dropped cookie on the floor. They also can read the emotions on your face and in your voice. And in your body language.

That's what Solo did that night in the warehouse. I thought I was reading him, but he was reading me.

But when we are training and searching, Solo needs to act and think independently. I need to help him use his good nose. That loving gaze is fine. After the job is done.

Dog and handler need to be together *and* separate. Bonded *and* independent. For some breeds and for some dogs, it's easier than for others.

And of course, that's true of us humans, too.

* * * * * * * * * * * *

Solo's reaction that night in the warehouse has been studied for more than a century. It's called the "Clever Hans effect" or the "Clever Hans phenomenon."

It doesn't happen just between dogs and people. Or people and people. The effect was named after a horse.

Hans was a smart German horse at the turn of the twentieth century. Crowds thought he was a genius. So did his math teacher owner.

Clever Hans could add, subtract, multiply, divide, and work with fractions. He could also read, spell, and tell time.

In September 1904 a commission created to investigate Hans came to its conclusion: Hans was the real deal. A horse genius. Newspapers worldwide compared Hans's math ability with that of a teenager's.

Hans's owner thought his horse knew complex
math and could read and spell.

But psychologist and scientist Oskar Pfungst set up a
series of experiments that finally led to the real answer:
Hans wasn't a genius but simply a clever, clever horse.
Pfungst showed that when no human watching knew the
correct answer, neither did Clever Hans. Or if the horse
couldn't see the person who knew the answer, he couldn't
get the right answer.

Hans was responding to numerous cues his owner
was giving him without realizing it: facial expressions,
tiny movements, a change in breathing. Hans could also
respond to cues the audience gave.

Researchers still use the term "Clever Hans" to warn of
the danger of unconsciously cueing an animal or a person
to do something you want.

• • • • • • • • • •

Despite the Pfungst report, many remained convinced that horses could be taught math and language skills.

There's no shortcut to reliability except constant, careful training. When I put Solo back in the car after that discouraging night in the warehouse, I joined Mike Baker at the other end of the hot, dusty building. He was working with a green handler learning how to methodically search storage shelves.

The little Malinois was already panting hard. At a certain point the hot, tired dog paused and started to lock in on a box with his nose, but Mike murmured, "Keep him moving."

A false alert avoided.

What might happen if drugs, or gunpowder, or a human bone are actually there, and a handler tries to move on?

The dog learns how to "commit," to plant herself stubbornly and ignore the handler's desire to move on.

It's not mystifying. It's not eerie. It is beautiful to see a dog trust her nose, and ignore her handler's efforts to get her to unstick herself from the flypaper scent that she's stuck to.

That's teamwork—not when a dog tries to please her human, but instead when she points her nose or paw or entire body at the scent, telling the handler, You idiot! It's here!

. . . .

CHAPTER NINETEEN

CLEVER HANS IN THE COURTROOM

That night in the warehouse wasn't the only time I fell for the Clever Solo effect.

When I first read about Clever Hans and his deluded owner and audience, I thought the story was so well known that experienced dog handlers would avoid that trap.

But Clever Hans has even managed to sneak into courtrooms across the nation and change the outcome of trials.

It starts innocently enough. A cadaver-dog handler brags at a seminar that her Doberman never false-alerts. A bloodhound handler says that his dog can follow a two-month-old track. Another claims that his coonhound can trail the scent of someone in a fast-moving car. For miles!

Some of that false bragging can end up as testimony in a courtroom. And when a dog handler claims that her dog is perfect and is never wrong, an innocent person can end up in prison.

Here is another weird thing about a lie: If it's repeated often enough, people start to think it's true. Even when, at the beginning, people knew it wasn't true.

Lies end up hurting more than the training of a particular dog. They aid in creating a harmful fiction about scent-detection dogs in general.

Roger Titus, vice president of the National Police Bloodhound Association, has handled and trained lots of bloodhounds over decades. His dogs have played a role in putting many guilty people behind bars.

But he is terrified of the lies he hears—both during trainings and on the witness stand. Those lies make dogs seem like superheroes.

● ● ● ● ● ● ● ● ● ● ●

Keith Pikett, a now-retired Texas sheriff's deputy, testified under oath that his bloodhounds' noses have almost never been wrong.

Sure, a little bit wrong. Even though Pikett doesn't keep detailed records, one bloodhound named Clue was wrong one time out of 1,659 times. Another bloodhound, James Bond, has been wrong one time out of 2,266 times.

The Innocence Project of Texas told the *New York Times* that between fifteen and twenty people went to prison "based on virtually nothing but Pikett's testimony."

Pikett's specialty was the scent lineup. A scent lineup starts when police investigators collect scent from a crime scene, then collect scent from a suspect. For instance, if police find a gun used in a shooting, they use cotton swabs to collect scent from the gun. Whoever used that gun probably left scent on it. And if the police have a per-

Photo by Cat Warren

Reward hug! Roger Titus praises a bloodhound for finding him.

son who they suspect used that gun, they collect scent from that person, too.

The dog's job is to match the scent from the crime scene with the scent of the suspect. It's incredibly hard to do without cross contamination or the Clever Hans effect coming into play. I watched videos online of Keith Pikett working his dogs, and I saw both.

Paint cans with numbers were placed on the grass in a line. An investigator pulled gauze pads in plastic bags out of one can and put them into another can with his bare hands. If there ever was an uncontaminated object with the suspect's scent on it, that scent was now possibly in several cans. Plus the investigator's scent was there too.

Pikett gave each bloodhound a scent object to sniff, then ran each of them on leashes down the line of paint cans. The dogs would look up, bay mournfully, and stop when Pikett stopped. They would shake their heads, slobber flying, and bay again.

They avoided some of the cans completely.

Pikett used the leash to stop one dog at a can. The dog stood there. Another dog paused right between two cans, and Pikett said the dog had alerted on one of the cans but not the other. One dog bayed and ran past two cans. Pikett said the dog had alerted on one of those cans.

Head shakes, barks, and pauses were all alerts, according to Pikett. The bloodhounds were doing all three of those things.

Even worse, what Pikett said they were doing—matching scent—was sending people to prison.

I was horrified. Nationally and internationally known trainers testified against Pikett—and against the system that allowed him to get away with this.

"This is the most primitive evidential police procedure I have ever witnessed," Robert Coote, the former head of a British K9 police unit, said after seeing the videos. "If it was not for the fact that it is a serious matter, I could have been watching a comedy."

The problem is that police, prosecutors, and juries across Texas believed Pikett's comedy for years. They loved him. He was confident and folksy on the witness stand, one Texas magazine reported.

And of course, his dogs were almost never wrong.

Juries are especially vulnerable to dog testimony, Roger Titus said. It makes sense. People like dogs. So they want to believe them. The problem is that we tend to forget that it's the handler at the other end of the leash who is testifying, and that the dog's "truthfulness" depends on the honesty and skill of the handler.

"Pikett has done a lot of damage to the

Pikett's claims about how fantastic his dogs were harmed many people.

veracity of dogs in the Texas system," Andy Rebmann said.

Pikett may be a lot like Clever Hans's owner.

Pikett's attorney told the *New York Times* in 2009 that his client's work with his dogs could seem mysterious. "The first time I saw it, I couldn't understand what the dogs were doing." But, he added, Pikett clearly knew.

"He's been doing it so long, he doesn't understand why we don't see it."

. . . .

Solo tries to be honest. Even so, Solo will false-alert. Like that night in the warehouse. That has to be logged in my training and search records. Every alert gets counted.

A false alert can happen when Solo smells scent but is not as close as he could and should get to the source. Nonetheless, he decides that's good enough for him.

It can happen if I do a bad job handling him, like I did in the hot warehouse.

But not always. Sometimes I'll never know why Solo alerted somewhere. Sometimes I can guess.

Once, we searched a junkyard of wrecked cars for a missing person, and Solo alerted on a front seat where an airbag had deployed and the windshield was shattered. He probably alerted on old blood from the accident.

If there are five or six cops standing and staring at something lying on the ground, say a bag with a dead animal in it? Solo will look at it too, look around, gauge everyone's expressions, and think, Hey, maybe that's something worth alerting on. They're into it, right?

In that case, I move on. During searches, if investigators want me to check garbage bags that look suspicious, or particular bones, to see if they might be human rather than animal, I politely ask if they can keep a short distance away.

On one search, I was having Solo check what I was sure was a pile of sand deposited by a recent creek flood, though one careful investigator thought it looked grave-like. I simply asked the searchers to stand away while I ran Solo through the area. They all obediently stepped well away and turned their backs, but they couldn't help looking over their shoulders to see what he would do. Solo sniffed and moved on.

Over the years, he has been increasingly proofed off dead animals and suggestive piles of dirt.

I've been proofed off being a sucker.

After reading about Clever Hans and Keith Pikett, and after reading a scientific study that showed how common it is to unconsciously cue our dogs, I also began changing some of my training habits.

I already knew from Suzie and Roy Ferguson how important it was not to anticipate finding something when you search.

On one training, I searched an entire abandoned aviation building where I hadn't placed a single hide. Solo yowled in protest as we left, trying to get at the tug toy in my pocket on the way out. He was mad at me.

Here he was, surrounded by guys in uniforms who love

to play tug. And no hides? My pocket got stained with resentful saliva on the way out, my thigh a bit bruised. He didn't false alert. It was a start.

The next time, the negative search would need to be "blind." I wouldn't know if hides were there or not. Then we'd move to "double blind." That would mean that the person who was with me wouldn't know if there were hides or not, or where they were placed. It would be a challenge for both me and Solo.

One step at a time.

I called David at home as the K9 unit left the aviation building. My patient husband put a cadaver hide out in the yard. As Solo and I walked from the car to the house, his head flipped. He ran toward the scent. Look! Cadaver after all! Give me my toy now. He was pleased.

So was I.

Solo was incredibly happy that he had found the training material without my giving him a command.

CHAPTER TWENTY

. . . .

E-NOSE

One week before Joan told me that Vita was pregnant with Solo, *Time* magazine ran a piece about the downfall of scent-detection dogs.

"Memo to man's best friend," *Time* magazine told its K9 subscribers. "In a few years, you may be relieved of your police drug-sniffing duties, thanks to a pair of Georgia Tech scientists."

Scientists, *Time* told scent-detection dogs, "have developed a handheld electronic nose that detects the presence of cocaine and other narcotics better than your cold, wet snout ever could."

I thought it was funny *Time* assumed that dogs could read magazines, but their noses weren't that great.

Maybe its editors assumed dog handlers would read the piece aloud to their dogs? I never read aloud to Solo, but maybe I wasn't giving him enough credit.

According to television, radio, magazines, and newspapers, dog nose substitutes weren't just hot. They were blowing dogs out of the scent business entirely.

What is an electronic nose? That term has been around for several decades. Electronic noses, or fake noses, as I prefer to call them, come in lots of different forms. But any electronic nose needs to do three things: take in a vapor, identify it, and then tell the machine's operator that the vapor is identified.

The dog's nose and olfactory system do something similar. They take in a smell and send a signal to the dog's brain. The dog sits because she's been trained to sit when she smells drugs. The handler sees his dog sitting and knows she's smelled drugs.

Researchers and manufacturers market their fake noses using familiar and fuzzy terms. The fake noses might not be surrounded by a warm furry snout, but the image needs to be there. So they come up with a bunch of doglike names for their mechanical noses: Fido, RealNose, the E-Dog.

Sometimes names backfire. "Sniffer dog on a chip" was a terrible choice.

All of these artificial noses—whether for bomb detection, drug detection, land-mine detection, or human-remains detection—are far superior to dogs, their boosters claim.

They won't shed. They won't bite. They won't get tired or overheated. They will detect parts per trillion of anything.

And they will put scent-detection dogs out of business. Any day now. . . .

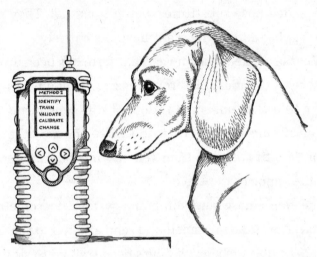

An e-nose and a dog's nose.

Most people like two things: new technology and dogs. I like certain kinds of technology. I love dogs. The e-nose seems like a winning combination. Because cool technology is news, and dogs have been around forever, perhaps we take dogs for granted.

Just a year and a half after *Time* magazine informed scent-detection dogs that they were working on borrowed time, I started Solo's serious training with Nancy Hook. I was able to read and understand his behavior changes. I was learning what happened to scent in heat, in wind, in rain, and in water. I was Dr. Dog Science.

At universities and in laboratories, researchers studied stuff like quantum biology. Others labored to understand what exact compounds in illegal drugs or in human remains made trained dogs recognize that particular smell.

A third group dismissed the dog's olfactory system altogether and continued to work on its replacement. Though the dog's nose remains a real challenge to reverse engineer, no scientific law says you can't try to build a better nose before you understand what's inside the original.

Mechanical noses have flourished in scientific competition. But some of the trash talk that goes on is silly. Anything a Georgia Tech engineer can do, an MIT researcher can do better. "There's no further improvement in the sensor part you can get," one MIT chemical engineer told *Wired* magazine about his e-nose creation in 2010. "It's the last word in sensors."

His e-nose may be the *latest* word in sensors. It's not going to be the last.

So which do I like better?

Unlike a canine, an electronic nose will keep working in heat and cold, never false alert, never get tired, never require dog kibble. It won't have to retire at the age of eight or nine.

To have an airport security employee thrust a cold metal electronic nose at me? Or have a friendly bomb dog do the same thing with his snout?

I greatly prefer a warm, wet nose.

. . . .

The problem with the majority of dog-nose replacements is that they don't have the skills that dogs have in one furry package. Remember when researchers in the 1970s tried to train pigs and wild animals to replace dogs? That didn't end well.

Machines probably aren't as aggressive as angry teenage raccoons, but they have their problems. Machines don't run themselves any more than dogs do. Machines break down and need constant adjustments. They can be more temperamental about weather than dogs are.

Well-trained scent-detection dogs are adaptable, mobile, and sensitive. They use a bunch of complex judgments to avoid false alerts. They can do several things: sniff, raise an alarm, bite if needed.

Best of all for those concerned about money, dogs are comparatively inexpensive. The argument that it takes money and time to train a dog is countered by the argument that training technicians on machines can be just as expensive.

"When I started doing work in this area twenty years ago, I originally thought we would be able to make a machine that could replicate a dog," said analytical chemist Ken Furton. "But it's not going to happen in my lifetime. We are not going to replicate what a dog can do."

The Pentagon came to the same conclusion in late 2010 in Afghanistan and Iraq. It shut down a huge program that had spent $17 billion on employees and technologies but had failed to make a dent in the problem of improvised explosive devices, or IEDs. Those handmade bombs have killed many thousands.

After five years, hundreds of projects, and a "blizzard of cash" paid to defense contractors, one system rose above the others—dogs and their handlers, along with observant people.

"The most effective IED detectors today . . . don't hum, whir, shoot, scan, or fly. They talk. And they bark," reported the Center for Public Integrity.

The rate of finding bombs with other technologies stood "stubbornly" at just 50 percent, one lieutenant general said. Handlers and dogs found IEDs at the rate of 80 percent. Lieutenant General Michael Oates said the best bomb detectors are dogs working with handlers, local informants, and the trained soldier's eye.

A few years ago, at a K9 training near a military base in North Carolina, I was standing near one of the best detection systems we currently have.

A special forces handler and his military working dog were taking a break from work in the Middle East. The Belgian Malinois was lying quietly beside his handler,

Corporal Sean Grady and Ace, an IED detection dog, pause briefly while sweeping for bombs during patrol in Iraq in 2012. The pair located sixteen IEDs in seven months.

with his back legs tucked under his haunches and his front claws dug slightly into the ground.

His eyes weren't fixed on his handler. Instead, the Malinois never stopped scanning the big field of mowed grass in front of them. The handler looked down at his dog. He told me it was like having an amazing extension, two and sometimes three hundred feet in front of you. His dog kept track of their surroundings and made sure his handler wasn't attacked. Or blown up.

The handler said he couldn't count the number of times his dog had saved his life.

. . . .

CHAPTER TWENTY-ONE

THE MONSTER MASH

Machines can be cool. But animal and machine mash-ups are marvelous.

A couple of decades before the electronic nose became commonplace, some army researchers, a lot like the ones at Southwest Research Institute in Texas who were playing with wild animals, thought about an even stranger way to replace the dog's nose.

It happened around the same time that other military researchers were realizing how good dogs were at a variety of jobs and began working on doing a better job of training dogs.

While the researchers at the US Army Limited War Laboratory knew that dogs were great at detecting the enemy and warning soldiers of an enemy's approach, the scientists wanted to see if they could make something smaller and more portable than a German shepherd.

So in 1965 they started working on an "insect ambush detector."

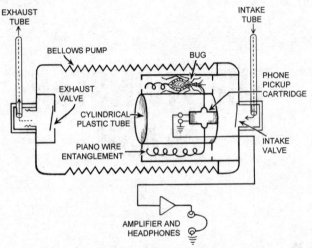

The researchers knew certain insects enjoy blood for breakfast, lunch, and dinner. Even for a snack. It makes sense that those insects want to find critters in their environment that have a lot of blood. We humans have quarts and quarts of it. If you weigh eighty pounds, you have almost three quarts of blood in you.

That was a nice insight, but the researchers had to narrow down the contenders. So they held insect tryouts.

Ticks, mosquitoes, bedbugs, and conenose bugs were the finalists.

All these insects use the warm breath of vertebrates to find their next meal. Next, researchers rigged up a plastic tube with a bellows and a sanded piano wire that twanged when the bugs' feet started a happy dance because they smelled food. A teeny microphone amplified their stomping foot music.

Ta-da. An "ambush detector," ready for a wild rumpus when it smelled the breath of enemy soldiers.

Early work narrowed down the best bugs for the job. When fleas sensed humans, they jumped violently. They couldn't settle down. They had to be fed too often. Bedbugs, like fleas, got overly excited thinking about a juicy meal.

Ticks were an early and interesting possibility. They love the smell of human breath and can move quickly. I've watched them crawling up my arm, so I know. They have soft feet. You think you can feel something crawling on you, but it's just a vague sense, and you forget about it. The next time you think about the tick is when someone tells you that something is attached to the back of your neck.

Soft feet are an advantage for ticks but not for the army researchers. Even with a microphone inside the detector, the device didn't pick up the sound. The researchers took the extra step of tying weights to the tiny tick feet, but they still couldn't twang the piano wire.

Conenose bugs—commonly known as kissing bugs because they most love the fleshy part of your face or lips for their bloodsucking—were ideal.

Until researchers tested them. The bugs performed miserably in field tests, the final army report noted. Once the conenose bugs got amped up, they were as bad as the bedbugs. They refused to settle down even when no one was there. Their feet just kept noisily sending out signals over the piano wire.

Fee-fi-fo-fum! We smell the blood of an American!

It got worse. The researchers realized it wasn't just the breath of vertebrates that made the bugs do the monster mash. Motion excited them. Wind excited them. Pretty much everything excited them. It was like a sleepover.

In what would become a standard excuse for not finding a system as good as a dog and handler, the final report said that using blood-loving bugs as sentries remained "technically feasible."

That term is a big ol' hairy clue for a failed experiment.

* * * * * * * * * * *

In the past decade the inventions that have truly turned on technology reporters aren't the hybrid machine-and-animal combinations, but plants. Like bionic spinach that gives off an infrared signal when it detects explosives.

Or bomb-detecting ferns.

"They turn completely white when they sense something nefarious around them," a Fox News reporter said.

And the big leafy plants are in malls and bars everywhere. No one pays any attention to them.

"It's very empowering because it will tell you that

there's an explosive around: 'Get the security guys here!'" biologist June Medford said about the ferns. And, she said, they have detection abilities that are similar to, or even better than, dogs.

The ferns sounded great.

So how long does it take them to turn white and tell the security guys to come running?

Hours.

Old-fashioned detection dogs, though, are pretty fast at telling us something is amiss. Faster than hours. Or a few minutes.

More like a few seconds.

When there's a bomb, time matters.

• • • • • • • • • • •

Bomb detection isn't the only arena where machines or mash-ups don't appear to be making much progress. The body-location business isn't seeing a great deal of electronic nose success either. Here's what a group of German forensic scientists said about using machines to locate human bodies (though they used dead rabbits in their experiment): "In principle, an electronic nose based on the sensors applied in this study can be used to find decomposing human bodies in terrain. However, for design and development of a practically applicable device, sampling and measurement procedures have to be optimized."

In principle, with optimized hooves, pigs can fly.

Between the Germans with their rabbits and other researchers who were testing wasps to see if they could find bodies, I felt better about the dog's place in the body-location universe.

Good dogs seem to move through a kind of complex decision tree on difficult searches: "This, not that," "Up, not down," and "That thing doesn't belong, but it's not what I'm looking for."

Nonetheless, challenges to the cadaver dog's nose are constant. No researcher ever wants to give up on the possibility that other species are better at scent detection than dogs. Perhaps it wouldn't be a machine but a bird that might do the trick? I worried when I first heard about the turkey vulture experiments in Germany.

"Not only can turkey vultures detect a dead mouse from more than 1,000 meters (3,300 feet) away, but they have a major advantage over sniffer dogs—they can fly, removing the challenge of difficult terrain," reported *Der Spiegel*, a German magazine, in 2011.

Turkey vultures appear to have the most advanced sense of smell of any raptor. The idea to use them to find human bodies seemed smart. I keep an eye on them during searches to see where they circle. A trained one would be like a search dog with wings and a better nose!

A German police commissioner told fascinated reporters that vultures, with their ability to fly high and cover huge stretches of forest, might have a major advantage over sniffer dogs. More than forty agencies from

Turkey vultures have an ultrasensitive olfactory system.

Photo by Don DeBold, Wikimedia (CC)

Switzerland, Austria, and Germany expressed interest.

It wasn't the first time people had thought about using vultures as sniffer animals. In the 1930s, oil industry engineers took a chemical that smells like dead animals and added it to huge pipelines snaking across Texas, then watched turkey vultures to see where the pipes leaked.

For this twenty-first-century German version of search vultures, a few small hurdles had to be overcome: The vultures needed to be properly trained, equipped with GPS locators, and encouraged to find only dead people, not dead animals. Once they found a victim, they had to be trained not to eat them before police arrived.

Vulture trainer German Alonso told reporters that police probably could arrive in their cruisers before too much important evidence went down the vultures' gullets. The birds tend to peck rather than devour.

Alonso's search vulture in training, Sherlock, didn't like to fly when he was searching for his training material. Instead he waddled around like a duck.

He was so anxious and antisocial, Alonso said, that when given the command to search, he hid in the woods or bolted.

Miss Marple and Columbo, two younger vultures brought in to assist Sherlock and make him feel as though he were part of a big vulture family, fought constantly. None of the vultures seemed to give a fig about the difference between animal carcasses and human cadavers.

By the time the laughter faded, so had the hope that turkey vultures were trainable for this particular task.

The vultures, a spokesman told a reporter, were no longer available for interviews.

CHAPTER TWENTY-TWO

. . . .

BOSS OF THE BOAT

David and I heard Nancy Hook muttering in the kennels as we waited for her. She was feeding dogs so all of us could get on the road faster. Our offering to help only slowed her down.

Next to the kennels, an old bass boat sat on a rusty trailer hitched to Nancy's pickup. Dozens of tiny weeds sprouted inside the boat. I pulled them absentmindedly until Nancy arrived and told me she was growing them on purpose. A recent rain had left an inch of murky water in the boat. I offered to bail it out. Nancy said a bit of water wouldn't sink us.

So off we drove, trailer bouncing, to Taylors

Millpond. Two women, a man, a dog, and a boat.

I'd heard stories about water-cadaver dogs helping locate bodies far below the surface. At first the stories had sounded like tall tales. But bodies do the same thing in water that they do on land: They decompose and send off gases. In the water, no matter how far down the body is, those compounds bubble up to the surface and hit the air.

Good water-cadaver dogs can be invaluable in searches. Lakes or rivers can veil a body even when searchers have the latest sonar equipment on hand. And lots of rivers and lakes across the US can be muddy or murky from flooding or algae. Divers can't see their hands in front of their faces.

Sending a diver into opaque water with snags or dangerous currents, based on a poorly trained dog's alert, isn't just a waste of time. It's endangering living people to recover someone who is dead.

Solo was now seven. In the not-too-distant future, his increasing knowledge would no longer counterbalance his aging body. But as long as he kept his good nose, water-cadaver work might extend his search life.

That was why Nancy was pushing us onto the water. She was right. I'd turned down a healthy handful of water searches, and I hated saying no.

But Solo wasn't trained for water cadaver. And neither was I. While the scent that dogs are looking for is the same on land or in water, the search itself is entirely different.

Water work depends on being able to know and read your dog, and having someone along who can watch for small behavior changes. Shelly Burton trains her cadaver dog, Mi'ja, on the water, with Joe Mayer's help, while Danny Holley drives the boat.

* * * * * * * * * *

A few miles down the road from Nancy's farm, Taylors Millpond is more like a lake than a pond. It has a small general store with a porch where men drink beer. We nodded hello. I tried to hand the store manager the two-dollar fee for launching the boat, but she shook her head silently. She knew Nancy.

Solo, bored, had already swum several laps across one end of the pond by the time we got the boat into the pond. Now he leaped on board, spraying water over Nancy and David. Solo loved boats. He thought it was fun to jump into them, and even more fun to jump out of them. I laughed. I was mostly dry from the waist up.

The boat rocked woozily as I pushed us off and got settled. A dripping Solo clambered over me, soaking me, to get to the prow.

David fiddled with the boat motor. It wouldn't start. He scowled.

"It was free," Nancy reminded him.

Finally the motor sputtered, coughed up an oily black cloud, and settled into a steady gurgle: "*Flubba, flubba, flubba.*"

The boat crawled away from the landing and toward the center of the huge pond, dotted with floating islands of lily pads.

On one side of the pond a great blue heron rose up out of the pine trees. Crappie, bullhead, bass, and catfish lurked beneath the lily pads and swam among the swamp tree roots.

A belted kingfisher knew where the fish were. She

A belted kingfisher watching for her next meal.

perched on a snag, her outsize head held still as she watched the calm water for her prey.

At our approach, she dropped off the snag and flew along the shore, chittering in irritation.

. . . .

In one way, working on water is like working on land— the dog needs to find the strongest source of scent.

Here's the problem: the dog is stuck on a boat.

But there's a solution: the dog learns how to boss around the boat driver, so that the driver goes where the dog wants to go.

How can he do that? Once the dog detects cadaver odor, if he sticks his head way over the right side of the boat, the driver knows to turn right. If the dog heads to the back of the boat, the driver knows he needs to turn the boat around and return to the area.

It sounds simple. But Solo and I were landlubbers. Neither of us fully understood what we were doing on water. We'd already been out in a boat with Nancy a number of times.

I tried to understand the currents, the wind, the movement of scent, the zigzag of the boat. I thought keeping a search pattern was hard on land. Water search patterns made me dizzy.

Solo wasn't much better. It takes patience and nerve strength on the dog's part to work on water. Solo has a great deal of drive and good nerve strength. He's not patient.

The first three times we went out, Solo yowled constantly, even when we were a hundred yards away from the scent source. He lunged in frustration for his tug toy, which I had stupidly stowed in the breast pocket of my life preserver.

Solo detected scent, just not the strongest scent. I threw my hands up. Nancy laughed and shook her head. Around the lake we went once more.

Dogs have to learn a whole range of new behaviors in a boat. A water-cadaver dog needs to give increasingly strong cues to the handler as the scent gets stronger. Solo, working on land, can run to where the scent is strongest and lie there.

And he can work out problems on his own timetable, not that of a moving boat.

Photo by Nancy Hook

Neither Solo nor I took to water work immediately.

• • • • • • • • • • • •

Andy Rebmann wrote much of the *Cadaver Dog Handbook*, but Marcia Koenig, his wife and a fellow cadaver-dog handler and trainer, wrote the chapter on water cadaver.

I read and reread it. I studied the illustrations. I watched dogs work on water.

Scent aside, dogs—and their handlers—face real challenges in water work. Solo and I were training on a large, calm pond. But searching on water is often dangerous. Especially when flooding, fast currents, and logjams are part of the mix.

Marcia researched and then wrote about an extraordinary search using dogs on a flooded Ohio River. She has a couple of theories about working on rivers, or with current. One is that dogs tend to alert where water breaks around an object. That makes sense because it can work a bit that way on land: trees or obstacles can help capture or trap scent.

The other insight was unique to river work.

The handlers looking for a drowning victim on the huge river all saw their dogs react in a similar way, though each dog had different body language.

Nikki, a German shepherd, had a reaction that her handler had never seen: her bottom jaw vibrated as she worked scent. At that point they were still nearly a mile and a half downstream from the victim. As the boat got closer and closer to the body, Nikki gulped water, spat it back out, clawed, and tried to jump into the water.

But when the boat crossed an invisible scent line, just upstream of where the body was located, she visibly relaxed. She smelled nothing but fresh, unscented water. "Nikki went completely limp for just an instant." Scent, scent, more scent . . . no scent.

Nikki's handler dropped a buoy at that line. She remembered thinking, "What have I done?"

For the dogs, Marcia wrote, "It was like stepping from one room to another."

That threshold was exactly where they found the victim, trapped under logs.

● ● ● ● ● ● ● ● ● ● ●

Scent can travel for miles down a river, or far across a lake or reservoir. Currents under a seemingly placid surface can move bodies great distances from where the victim fell in.

And water searches on large bodies of water can have a three-dimensionality that makes it difficult or impossible to locate a body, even using the latest technology and divers. Side-scan sonar can help create an image of the floor of a lake or ocean, but if you've got a search area as large as a reservoir, seeing a victim can be like seeing a needle in a haystack: it's difficult to tell the difference among boulders, logs, bushes, snags—and a body. The victim can also be suspended between the bottom and the surface because of current or temperature differences in the water.

Large lakes and reservoirs become huge and forbidding areas to search, almost like outer space.

Roy and Suzie Ferguson of Tennessee know these difficulties firsthand.

The victim was last seen covering her boat on a long dock off a huge Tennessee lake. She simply disappeared. Searchers worked nearly nonstop for two weeks around the dock area, with sonar, with deep-water cameras. They dragged and dove. Nothing.

Investigators started to wonder whether the victim had simply left the dock. Or whether it was murder. It's a natural reaction. There was no way of knowing what had happened to her. They couldn't imagine she was in the lake.

After two weeks, when police and divers ran out of options, they called in two dogs from Roy and Suzie Ferguson's Tennessee team.

The dogs alerted on the dock, right where the victim was last seen. Her family didn't want to give up. They brought in an underwater construction crew with a deep-water robot from out of state.

Roy and Suzie Ferguson came this time, along with the original two team members and their dogs. Suzie brought her German shepherd, Schatzie.

Roy was in charge of watching the dogs and handlers work. It's always valuable on land searches if someone is there who knows how dogs react on land. Having a person who knows how dogs react to scent on water—which can be subtle—is invaluable.

So Roy watched the dogs' alert patterns as they worked from boats and off other docks for two days. He created a map that showed where all the dogs showed the most interest. They had narrowed a huge search area to a twenty-by-forty-foot oval.

The construction crew dropped the little submersible robot, with its camera and sonar, into the water right in the middle of that oval. The water was remarkably clear. In less than two minutes, the operators saw the victim, caught in the eye of the robot's camera.

She was about thirty feet out from where she last was seen alive, covering her boat. That was in one dimension. She was also two hundred thirty feet down. That's about the height of a twenty-story skyscraper.

She managed, nonetheless, to send a final clear signal to the dogs.

CHAPTER TWENTY-THREE

. . . .

THE DOGS OF PEACE

Dogs have been used during war for thousands of years. In ancient Egypt and Greece, huge mastiff-like dogs attacked enemy soldiers. The Romans used sentry and patrol dogs. In the eighteenth century, Frederick the Great of Prussia had messenger dogs ferry battle instructions and news to the front lines.

A different focus for war dogs emerged in the nineteenth century. Several European countries started using dogs to find and save the wounded after battle. By World War I, Red Cross dogs commonly carried saddlebags filled with alcohol, water, and medical supplies to wounded soldiers.

POLICE DOG   BELGIAN SHEPHERD

Illustration by Louis Agassiz Fuertes, 1919

Ambulance dogs on the battlefield.

The Germans used German shepherds, of course. The English used a mixture of breeds—from Airedales to collies to mutts. No matter what side they were on, these dogs became famous as "mercy dogs" or "ambulance dogs." At one point during World War I, the Red Cross estimated that ten thousand dogs were on the front, though that's probably a wild guess on the high side. But dogs were great mascots for the Red Cross.

Mercy dogs dealt only with the living. "Dogs are never trained to scent out the dead," wrote Ellwood Hendrick in a 1917 issue of the *Red Cross Magazine*. "Their business is to assist the wounded."

Even at disaster scenes today, we prioritize finding the living before trying to recover bodies.

But recovering the remains of soldiers who die in war has long been an emotional and political issue. Families and friends of those killed and missing can feel anguish and doubt for decades when there are no remains to bury, or no concrete evidence of their loved one's death.

Training dogs to scent the dead wouldn't happen until many decades later, in the mid-1970s. And it wouldn't be until the twenty-first century that anyone in the United States considered using cadaver dogs to find missing soldiers.

It would be a former marine who would lead the way.

• • • • • • • • • • • •

When Matt Zarrella was a boy, he struggled with dyslexia. Words and letters reversed themselves on the page as he stared at them. He also had energy to burn. He was constantly in trouble. His family's dogs were his love and his escape.

As a young man, Matt found a home in the marines and then with the state police. The only thing missing from work? Dogs.

So when Matt was a young state trooper, he went to his unit's captain. He told him he wanted to train a search-and-rescue dog for the Rhode Island State Police.

His captain said there was no money for that, and said if Matt wanted to do it, he had to do it on his own time.

So Matt, who was stubborn, took Hannibal, his one-hundred-thirty-pound greater Swiss mountain dog, to someone who he thought could help him.

Andy Rebmann had recently retired from the

Connecticut State Police. He and his dogs were now famous across the Northeast and beyond for finding people, alive or dead. Many considered him the best search-dog trainer in the country. And Connecticut, where he still lived, was just right up the road from Rhode Island.

Andy thought Hannibal showed promise. The Swiss dogs were bred as draft dogs, to pull carts and sleds in mountain villages, not to track missing people. But Hannibal, like Matt, was stubborn and filled with energy.

So when Matt got time off, he drove north to train with Andy. For nearly a year Hannibal learned how to be a trailing dog instead of a draft dog. The same week Hannibal certified, he found a missing teenager alive. Then he learned to be a cadaver dog.

Hannibal helped located ten bodies and found two missing people alive during his search career.

By then the Rhode Island State Police decided that a K9 program might be a good idea after all. Matt founded their program and started working with other officers and other dogs. Most of the dogs were adopted from shelters. When the dogs were adopted, many of them were only days or hours away from being euthanized—usually because of their impossible levels of energy.

The barracks for the state police slowly filled with shelter dogs in training running madly around, stealing old slices of pizza off desks in their spare time and finding lost people when they were on the job.

If you are good at something, word tends to spread. Matt and his dogs got a reputation.

One day in 2002, Matt got an interesting phone call. Might cadaver dogs be effective in helping recover missing servicemen in Vietnam? The retired military officer on the phone questioned Matt at length. What would they need to get such a program started? What would the handlers need? The dogs need?

The conversation moved in an obvious direction.

"It just came down to asking me if I would do it. I was extremely honored," Matt said. He had been a marine, and their motto is "Leave no one behind."

Matt would be the first cadaver-dog handler to officially search for missing soldiers from any US conflict.

It was a scary assignment. Matt and his two German shepherds from the comparatively cool Northeast would fly to the jungles of Vietnam to look for remains of soldiers who disappeared decades before.

Matt called Andy. Matt adores and respects Andy, and Andy considers Matt the equivalent of an adopted son. They talked about whether one of Matt's dogs, Panzer, was too old to go. Gunner, Matt's middle-aged Swiss mountain search dog, had gotten cancer and had a leg amputated after Matt had committed to going to Vietnam. Gunner couldn't go.

But Matt couldn't back out. He'd promised the military two dogs. So he rushed to the pound and found a

Matt's family dog Hannibal became
his first search-and-rescue dog.

six-month-old German shepherd. The pound had labeled
him "aggressive."

Maximus wasn't mean. He did have a ton of energy.
Matt trained him hard over the next six months. But the
one thing he couldn't do was make Max age faster.

• • • • • • • • • • •

When Matt flew to Vietnam with his two cadaver dogs, nearly two thousand servicemen were still missing in Vietnam. And Matt had a one-year-old dog and a nine-year-old dog—positioned at the extreme ends of the age spectrum for search dogs. Max was just certified. Panzer was highly experienced, but old and soft enough to tire quickly or even possibly die in the extreme search conditions.

Matt wondered if he were setting up his own dogs to fail. He knew Panzer could find the dead and the buried. She'd done it for years in the Northeast. But the oldest buried remains she'd found were a decade old, not nearly four decades old, as they would be in Vietnam.

The temperatures and conditions would be unfamiliar and grueling. Panzer worked in snow and ice, but mangrove swamps and rice paddies with high humidity and heat indexes above one hundred degrees would be new territory.

The mission to find servicemen missing in action in Vietnam had added urgency. Witnesses to fighter jets that had been shot down during the height of the conflict in the 1960s were dying. Recovery efforts had slowed. Fewer and fewer US servicemen's remains were being found.

Captain David Phillips's fixed-wing fighter jet had been shot down on July 3, 1966, in a thicket of mangrove trees near a poor, tiny village.

A witness told authorities that he had recovered Phillips's remains and buried them. The jet had been entirely repurposed.

Matt, with Panzer on the right and Max on the left, arrived in Vietnam to unfamiliar search conditions.

It was acidic soil. Bones would disappear—if they had been there in the first place.

The search went quickly once the helicopter holding Matt and his dogs landed.

Panzer alerted on the exact spot where a villager said he had buried the remains, near his home. That was nice confirmation, but military anthropologists had planned to dig there anyway.

Matt couldn't help thinking that might not be the end of the story. So he and Panzer wandered toward the back of the house and the thick jungle at the outskirts of the village.

They moved toward an old family cemetery and then to a garbage dump about a hundred fifty feet away from the site where witnesses said Phillips was buried.

That was when Matt saw Panzer's body language change. She eyed Matt. She threw her head up. She worked hard in a small area but didn't give a final alert.

Panzer was tired. Matt gave her water and got young Max.

Max did the same thing Panzer had, in the same area. Except Max gave his final alert.

"He was sure it was there. It was in his eyes."

Matt went to talk to two of the anthropologists, who were intrigued by the dogs' work. In a jungle, one hundred fifty feet is a long distance.

Matt and his dogs flew to other sites. Some sites would be burials; some would be crash sites; some would be spots where prisoners of war had reportedly died in

Air Force Captain David J. Phillips Jr.

camps and been buried by villagers; some sites were entirely invented by the locals.

· · · · · · · · · · ·

Nearly a month later Matt was in the lobby of his Vietnam hotel and ran into one of the anthropologists from the Phillips site. Matt and the dogs had just finished their last case. They'd found nothing that could be clearly identified as human remains.

Matt felt terrible.

"Did anyone tell you what we recovered at the site you searched?" the anthropologist asked him. Matt had heard nothing.

The anthropologists had excavated the general area where Max had alerted and Panzer had shown interest.

Six inches down they found a pocketknife. A zipper from a flight suit. Pieces of life support equipment. And what the anthropologist thought was a human kneecap, although that hadn't yet been confirmed.

"I wanted to break down and cry," Matt said.

The grueling trip halfway around the world for Matt and his two dogs hadn't been in vain.

CHAPTER TWENTY-FOUR

. . . .

WATER WITCH

By the time the United States invaded Iraq in 2003, the military knew dogs were invaluable for bomb- and land-mine detection, sentry duty, and enemy tracking and capture.

And because of the more recent experience at the disaster sites of 9/11, the military knew that good cadaver dogs could help find the missing and dead.

In 2009, only a few service people were missing from the conflicts in Iraq and Afghanistan. But this time, unlike the Vietnam War, the US military was not going to leave them behind.

Kathy Holbert runs a kennel in the mountains of Barbour County, West Virginia. Self-sufficient and humorous, she trains detection and patrol dogs, boards people's pets, and breeds a variety of working dogs, including German shepherds and Beaucerons, an ancient French herding breed.

Kathy was in the military, first as a parachute rigger and then as a dog handler. Her first dog, a German shepherd named Dick, bit her a number of times during training. Not usually on purpose.

"I was a terrible, terrible handler," she said. "My timing was awful. They used to use me to show handlers how not to do things."

That's hard to believe. Watching Kathy work with both dogs and handlers makes the work seem straightforward and low-key.

When Kathy got a call about going to the Middle East in June 2009, she was working her second cadaver dog, Strega, a sable German shepherd with an extra-long tail, big ears, and a mature intelligence. *Strega* means "witch" in Italian.

Because Kathy—along with her grandfathers, her father, her brother, and her husband—had served in the military, she said yes.

Getting off the plane in September in Iraq felt like a body blow. "It's hard to describe the heat. It's like having a blow-dryer in your face." A blow-dryer that smells like urine and blows sand at you.

Kathy put booties on Strega, but they sometimes melted. The temperatures in Iraq can average above one hundred ten degrees in September. Instead of trying to escape the

Temperatures in Iraq were brutal, and Kathy
was careful to keep Strega well hydrated.

heat, Kathy decided to embrace it. She stayed outside with
Strega as much as she could. They both adjusted.

Strega worked steadily. Not too fast, not too slow.
She had plenty of drive, but she didn't show it off. Those
qualities served her and Kathy well.

Searching for human remains in Iraq was hard—both
physically and emotionally. Many of their searches were
after a bomb had exploded. The scent of death was both
everywhere and nowhere, like at disaster scenes. Strega's
searches in West Virginia had been different. In Iraq, she
needed to keep searching for any trace of someone that
could be found after an IED had gone off.

But Kathy knew what those searches meant to the victims' family and friends.

Strega adjusted to very different search conditions in Iraq.

And soon enough, Strega understood the job as well. She started finding the little that remained.

* * * * * * * * * * *

After their arrival in Iraq in September 2009, Kathy and Strega started to adjust to the oppressive heat, the wind, and the sand.

In November, just two months after their arrival, the US military flew them to Afghanistan, fifteen hundred miles to the east.

As they came in, Kathy could see the country's beauty below, its glorious tan-and-ocher mountains, its winding rivers, its farms and orchards.

But Kathy knew the beauty would be offset by what

she and Strega would face on landing—a harsher and even more dangerous environment than in Iraq.

"Afghanistan was different," she said flatly. "They try to kill the dogs."

Military K9s and handlers get targeted in Afghanistan more than in Iraq. Taliban fighters know how bad it feels to US servicemen when they lose a handler or K9.

Kathy keeps a long list of dogs and handlers killed there.

It's not only the Taliban and their sympathizers who pose a danger. In Afghanistan, Strega was just another occupier. Children, mostly girls, followed Kathy and Strega after they landed. Kathy turned to greet the girls and hand them candy. They countered by throwing rocks at Strega.

Soon Kathy and Strega were in a convoy, heading north to a search in the Murghab River, near the border of Turkmenistan.

Two paratroopers had drowned. It was a classic tragedy—a crate of supplies dropped out of an aircraft by parachute ended up in the river instead of onshore.

The first paratrooper was in full battle dress. He waded out onto the shelf of the river, where the water was calm and shallow, and grabbed the supply crate as it floated by. He must have been pulled hard off the shelf's rim just as the crate plunged into the fast, deep water.

Seeing his friend in trouble, another trooper went in to save him. Then he was gone too.

The Taliban, downriver from the site, lied and claimed that they had both men's bodies.

US Navy personnel search the Murghab River for the drowned paratrooper.

Thus began a massive recovery operation for the two deceased men.

After a week of searching, British soldiers found the paratrooper who had tried to rescue his friend. His body was around the bend in the river, well downstream from where the men had gone in.

The recovery operation came at great cost. The area down the river was filled with Taliban fighters.

No second body surfaced. That was when Greg Sanson, an advisor for US forces in Iraq, got a call asking for a human-remains-detection dog team. He sent Kathy and Strega.

In Afghanistan the terrain was steep, with willows along the edge of the river. The water looked calm on its east side, where it was shallow and reflected the blue sky. Farther out the water turned greenish gray as it churned and frothed.

Kathy suggested to the military team that she and

Strega start their search at the place where the men had fallen in. The team said they were sure the current had moved the victim beyond the bend of the river.

Kathy respectfully asked again if they might start at the point where the victim was last seen.

So that's what they did. Kathy started Strega at ten a.m. on the east bank of the river, where it was warmer in midmorning, with a current that moved scent around. It wasn't just the river that was dangerous. A sheep-and-goat guard dog—powerful and leggy—headed straight for them. He stopped at the last moment, then retreated to a ridge above the river. He weighed at least a hundred twenty-five pounds.

"He watched the whole time we worked," Kathy said.

Strega worked her way back to the bend, where the military suspected the paratrooper's body had gone. Then she tried to get into the river. She had no interest in going farther around the bend. She moved back upriver toward the rapids.

She alerted on the shore, straight across from a churning area where the men were last seen. It was her simple alert. A sit.

It told Kathy everything she needed to know, although she suspected that the divers, who had never worked with a dog, probably hoped for more "yippie-yi-yo-ki-yay."

Strega was not a dog who did backflips. Her sit, nonetheless, changed everyone's thinking about where the paratrooper's body might be.

The next day was a Sunday. It wasn't a day of rest. The humidity and wind were better for scent, and Strega once again told everyone she was pretty darned sure the victim's body had never made it past the bend in the river. She kept working upriver, closer and closer to the whirling rapids.

The divers rigged a complex system, a high line over the river, and put Kathy and Strega on a rubber raft. They moved the raft back and forth across the river on the line.

Strega alerted right over the rapids, midway across the river. Kathy and the divers looked down to see a deep undercut. The water there looked as though it were boiling.

A hydraulic boil is like a washing machine in spin cycle with lots of water. It keeps spinning clothes around but never lets them escape. It's also called a "drowning machine."

Photo courtesy of Kathy Holbert

Strega's alert.

The divers tried to search in the boil, but the currents were too strong. They did manage to snag the original parachute and cargo box. Both had been trapped inside the boil.

The recovery team had to trust Strega. People had already died attempting to find the first victim.

Although the military talked about a couple of

A DROWNING MACHINE

Hydraulic boils are dangerous for anyone who falls into a rapid river, or goes in right below a dam. The force of water dropping from one level to another makes the water circulate over itself in a churning motion. Kayakers with lots of experience know how to push to the bottom of the river and slip out underneath the boil!

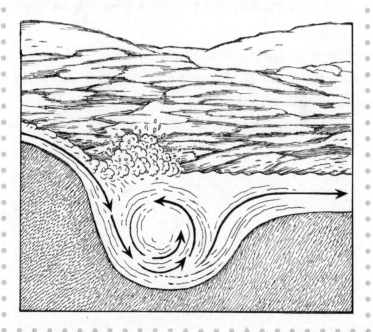

different options—including putting some blasts into the river—they decided to let nature take its course.

Strega had worked for three separate days and told them the same thing each time.

The recovery team told the villagers there would be a reward if they watched the river. Kathy provided the military with her estimate of when villagers might see something, given the days since the paratrooper disappeared, what he wore, and the water temperature.

The hydraulic boil made it hard to know what might happen.

In late November, nearly two weeks after the search ended, villagers contacted the military. The paratrooper's body had surfaced—right in the area where Strega alerted.

Strega, a dog trained to find the dead, had probably helped save lives. The Taliban didn't get the body, and no one else died on that mission.

No one triumphed, either.

CHAPTER TWENTY-FIVE

· · · · · · · · · · ·

ON WOLF STREET

When I walk in the North Carolina woods with Solo and he slows to investigate a particular scent, I wonder whether it's more than squirrel pee or the ancient track of a pit bull.

When I think about who might lie beneath the forest floor, my perspective shifts. The South's dead go back many thousands of years.

One day we were called to search an abandoned plantation for a missing person. Solo sniffed and worked the downhill side of a small slave cabin at some length. He didn't give his final down alert. I watched him and realized that his interest probably didn't relate to the missing person we were looking for.

But as I drove home, exhausted, I couldn't get that sad slave quarters out of my mind. How much birthing, living—and perhaps even dying—must have occurred in that cabin.

On another search, investigators spent an hour pulling a mound of stones near a pond apart, based on Solo's and another dog's alerts. But when they got down to ground level and found roots that clearly had been there longer than two years, they didn't go deeper. If someone was buried farther down, it wasn't the victim we were looking for.

I remain curious about that mound of stones. It overlooked a pond in the middle of those woods.

The search for what are called "historic human remains" has become more sophisticated over the last decade. People are using family records, land deeds, oral and written history—and dogs.

Well-trained cadaver dogs have been used to discover or narrow down what are open-air museums: abandoned cemeteries, little-known battle sites, and archaeological sites.

· · · · · · · · · · ·

A famous bloodhound trainer, Bill Tolhurst, was involved in one of the first documented cases where dogs were used to find ancient remains. In 1987 he took his chocolate Labrador, Candy, to a site in Ontario, Canada, where construction workers had found a skull. Archaeologists soon realized that the remains were from the War of 1812, when the US invaded Canada. Bill and Candy helped them locate three additional skeletons.

GRAVE WORK

It's hard work to find historic human remains that can be hundreds of years old and often lie in unmarked graves. But lots of tools help. Here are a few of them. Can you think of others?

• Soil samples that can be tested for the compounds found in historic human remains

• Old letters or oral history (stories that get passed on to each generation)

• Ground-penetrating radar that can show old burials or soil changes many feet below the surface

• The family Bibles that some early families in the US used to kept track of birth, marriage, and death records

• And of course, a cadaver dog trained to find historic human remains!

Several cadaver-dog teams across the country now specialize in old burials. A few of them are starting to get consistent—and verifiable—results.

But just like with complex criminal cases, it often takes a knowledgeable group of specialists and equipment, along with scent-detection dogs, to find historic remains.

Using dogs to find ancient human remains is more controversial than using them for more recent deaths. Since no one has established exactly what compounds cause dogs to recognize human remains, ancient graves raise even more questions.

The Biblical saying "Dust thou art and unto dust thou shalt return" has a scientific basis. At some point most of us rejoin the earth so completely that we're not easily distinguishable from the ground around us.

That process can take a long, long time. Depending on the surroundings, the climate, and the kind of preservation used for the body, it can take thousands of years.

How far back can the dog go? Without hesitating, Solo alerted on an eight-hundred-year-old bone from the Mississippi Delta. I've watched many cadaver dogs do the same.

When I watch well-trained cadaver dogs define the outer edges of old cemeteries—throwing their heads; staring up into the trees, even putting their feet up to try to climb them; and bringing their noses deep down into tree roots growing out of depressions in the earth—I'm fascinated.

I tread more lightly in those spots.

• • • • • • • • • • • •

In the last months of the Civil War, a panicked Confederacy, terrified of Union General William Sherman's advance through Georgia, shipped five thousand Union prisoners from the notorious Andersonville prison camp south of Atlanta to a tiny town more than a hundred miles farther south—Thomasville, Georgia.

Slaves there were ordered to dig long trenches, six to eight feet deep and ten to twelve feet wide, to create the boundaries of a five-acre camp prison in the piney woods. Shortly after, the Andersonville prisoners, ill and starving, started arriving. And dying.

The lot on Wolf Street in Thomasville that once held thousands of Union soldiers is tiny. Less than an acre of the original prison is still undeveloped, a patch of scrubby grass with a few pines and oaks. A small historical marker notes the spot's significance, but the marker is darkened with age, and the lot is shaded. I found only one obscure guidebook that included its presence. That's in comparison with the hundreds of mentions of Thomasville's glories: its huge oak tree in downtown that dates back to 1680, and its even larger vacation homes built by wealthy industrialists in the nineteenth century.

The idea of bringing in cadaver dogs to help establish whether Civil War prisoners were buried on Wolf Street started when assistant city manager Kha McDonald, born and raised in Thomasville, Georgia, realized that she wanted to know more about that scrubby site with its small plaque.

Her hometown had avoided the worst damage from the Civil War, but mysteries remained. Hundreds of Union dead were unaccounted for. Where were the prisoners buried who had died during treatment at the Methodist church? Was there a mass grave near or at the Wolf Street site?

That uncertain history was part of Kha's own legacy in a town built on slavery. At one time the enslaved population outnumbered the white population in Thomasville.

"You can't escape that," Kha said.

And the prison camp, where five hundred prisoners had reportedly died, barely registers as a blip in the history of Thomasville or the Civil War. Even though, after the war, the federal government made the most sustained effort in the history of the country to unbury, identify, and rebury Union soldiers in federal cemeteries, this effort missed Thomasville entirely.

That's not surprising. Estimates of men who died during the war are as high as 750,000. As historian J. David Hacker noted, "Men went missing; battle, hospital and prison reports were incomplete and inaccurate; dead men were buried unidentified; and family members were forced to infer the fate of a loved one from his failure to return home after the war."

Dogs, Kha learned, were being used in the Mississippi Delta to find human remains from the mound-building civilizations that had once lived there, remains that were eight hundred to twelve hundred years old. So Kha got in touch with two handlers: Lisa Higgins from Louisiana and Suzi Goodhope, who lived just across the Georgia border in Florida.

Searching for historic human remains wasn't an obvious choice for Lisa. She had plenty of criminal and missing persons cases to deal with—and a demanding seminar schedule. Lisa also admitted to me that in the beginning she was deeply skeptical that even well-trained cadaver dogs were capable of detecting ancient remains.

She was converted—partly by watching her own dogs, partly by watching other top handlers work their dogs.

Lisa Higgins's cadaver dog Dixee does her sit alert
in a shallow depression in an old cemetery in rural
Indiana that has many unmarked graves.

And in several instances she has received clear confirmation from excavations.

So Lisa brought her two dogs, Dixee and Maggie, to Thomasville. Suzi brought her two Belgian Malinois, Temple and Shiraz, or, as she calls them, "the guttersnipe and the princess." Temple is a shelter rescue probably only part Malinois. Nonetheless, she carries many of those genes: driven, opinionated, and hardheaded. Shiraz looks delicate and royal, but she's tough and stubborn.

Kha contributed her amateur historian's passion, as well as a geologist with ground-penetrating radar. The

Shiraz, one of Suzi Goodhope's Belgian Malinois, only looks dainty.

Thomas County Historical Society provided documents.

Looking for the long gone is not straightforward. We humans might think scent would be strongest down inside the rectangular depressions that seem to indicate where bodies are buried in old cemeteries. That isn't always the case.

As Lisa said, we can't know exactly where the dogs are smelling scent most strongly. Low spots gather more scent. Animal burrows can make the scent more accessible in one area rather than another. And scientists don't know why vegetation and roots seem to make cadaver scent more available. What's clear is that dogs appear drawn to vegetation and trees near a burial.

. . . .

On Wolf Street the dogs moved along the partly-filled-in ditch, sometimes slowing and alerting within a few feet of one another, in the same general area. Suzi lost count of the alerts.

Kha, watching the dogs work, saw a pattern. Suzi and everybody had "significant hits in the trench," she recalled.

Then the dogs would go over to the property line. One old tree with a hole in the bottom of it stands there. Every dog indicated enthusiastically on that hole, Kha said. They acted as if they'd "hit the glory land" and someone was "blowing the fumes up" from the earth beneath.

Then ground-penetrating-radar operators came in.

Using their machines, they confirmed odd changes in the soil below the scrubby grass, as well as soil changes in the ditch where Suzi had flagged dog alerts. These changes can often mean that the soil was dug, or filled there— perhaps for burials.

None of this is a certainty. But it's enough for Kha to find money to bring the tiny site out of the shade. Perhaps the town will add a fence or some markers.

If the massive oak tree in downtown Thomasville gets recognition for being one of the biggest oaks in the Southeast, if tourists come and tour the town's huge historic mansions, perhaps this humble site that marks the final days of Union prisoners in Thomasville will get some recognition.

CHAPTER TWENTY-SIX

• • • • • • • • • • •

THE BURIAL GROUNDS

Early-morning mist still hung above the Great Pee Dee River near the border of North and South Carolina. On a little wooded bluff overlooking the river was a lichen-covered stone, placed there sometime in the 1960s.

That stone represented hope—that this was the cemetery where Revolutionary War captain Claudius Pegues Jr. was buried. He died in 1792, less than a decade after the War of Independence was won.

Pegues had fought at the side of the wily Francis Marion. Marion, "the Swamp Fox," had led a group of backwoods soldiers against the British. Marion's troops had often attacked from the underbrush or marshes of a land they knew well. They'd also escaped that way.

The British had hated the Swamp Fox. "The Devil himself could not catch him," a British lieutenant had sworn.

The bluff we were standing on overlooked the once-massive Pegues family cotton plantation.

But perhaps Claudius Jr. wasn't there at all. A stone marker doesn't mean that someone is buried there.

Pegues's great-great-great-great-granddaughter Pat Franklin stood at the edge of the woods, her gray hair swept up in a loose knot. Pat hadn't known about cadaver dogs, but her longtime friend, area genealogist May MacCallum, had read about cadaver dogs helping find unmarked graves. Pat and May did some more research. Then they called Paul Martin of Tennessee, who specializes in old burials.

And Paul called me. Did I want to bring Solo? I was thrilled.

Pat didn't think that old family records, letters, wills, and oral history told the same story about where her ancestors were buried.

Her grandmother always told her "the old burying ground" was at the Charrows. That was where we stood now. Pat's grandmother, to prevent her from going into the woods as a child, told Pat that a coachwhip snake guarded the spot. They are long, fast, and smart, with large dark eyes, and scales that look like braided leather. The adults can reach eight feet long.

A fable claims a coachwhip will chase you, whip you

The eastern coachwhip snake is beautiful, fast, and smart—
with excellent vision.

to death with its tail, and then stick the tip of its tail up
your nose to make sure you're not breathing.

The reality is that they streak away as fast as they can
from humans. Guarding isn't their biggest strength.

Now Pat wanted to know where her ancestors lay.

* * * * * * * * * * *

Solo didn't know much about history. Or care. He whined
loudly in the car. He was a cemetery novice and would not
get to go first, which irritated him greatly.

Paul Martin would first run Macy, one of his veteran
cadaver dogs. Paul started researching ancient human
remains more than a decade before, and it has become
both an intellectual and training challenge for him.

It was probably still a bit too early and cold, he said.
There's a sweet spot when dogs are best able to detect the
scent of historic human remains. Once more sun penetrated

the winter understory, Paul said, the scent, if it was there, would start to rise and move. Too much sun burns it off.

Macy looks more like a cross between Old Yeller and Gollum than a Labrador. He's slippery and primitive, with amber eyes, a reddish-dun coat, and ribs sticking out. Though he eats constantly, he runs the calories off just as quickly. At the moment, he had raw spots on his pink nose from butting his wire crate door in his eagerness to get out.

Macy banged out a joyous tempo on the door as Paul approached his crate. As soon as Paul opened the door, Macy shot out into the woods.

Paul followed him slowly, then stood amid the oak, beech, sweet gum, black cherry, and sycamore trees. Calm and quiet, he watched Macy dash around the perimeter.

"Too far," he said in his nasal, lilting voice as Macy dropped off the bluff toward the river. It's a term that Lisa Higgins uses, and I had started using it with Solo. It doesn't mean "Come." It means "Start to circle back, but keep searching."

Macy worked hard, snorkeling scent in the leaves. He didn't find anything. Either it was too cold out or there was no human-remains scent to find.

Macy ignored Paul, didn't ask to be rewarded, and kept working.

After ten minutes Paul put him back into his crate. We would wait until the winter sun penetrated the tree canopy.

In the meantime another glade beckoned. It was warmer

than this hillcrest. Down the hill, past the fields of stubble where cotton was harvested months before, lay the African American cemetery—covered with periwinkle and brambles, and spotted with daffodils. It had stone headstones that dated up to 1910. Some of the rotted planks on the site may have come from slaves' headstones.

A number of former slaves had become tenant farmers after they'd been emancipated. They stayed on the plantation. They had little choice. Pat and May have worked to record this cemetery as well, but much less is known about it.

Paul turned to me. It was Solo's turn.

Solo could hardly wait to be freed from his backseat prison.

Photo by Cat Warren

Solo was ecstatic, whirling and barking sharply, coming back to hit my leg. I offered him water, since he panted in his excitement. He wasn't interested. He dashed down the hill, ignoring the rough cotton stubble, and into the woods and underbrush at the bottom. Scent must have called to him.

By the time we humans entered the woods, Solo was already working. He had never been exposed to gravestones, except for one hasty search of a modern cemetery. He had no reason to suspect they had any significance. Given how the stones were scattered and fallen, buried in bramble, or broken, they could be far from the deceased they were meant to identify.

Nonetheless, from twenty feet away I heard Solo almost gurgling as he tried to bring more scent into his nose. He did his down alert, staring at me. He was surrounded by periwinkle and daffodils. I saw several tilted headstones peeking out from under the vines.

"Reward him," Paul said. I did.

Solo alerted seven or eight times.

Paul estimated that at least seventy-five slaves, former slaves, and tenant farmers were buried here. Pat doesn't know how old the cemetery is.

One of the headstones near to one of Solo's alerts drew me in. It had a small mud dauber's nest on it but was in pristine condition. It read: "In Memory of Furby Pegues. Wife of Sharper Pegues. Born May 22, 1838. Died Dec. 24, 1881."

Who was she? I won-
dered later. And her hus-
band, Sharper? Her birth
date and both of their last
names, those of the plan-
tation owners, told me
that they both must have
been slaves.

But Furby died well
after President Abraham
Lincoln's Emancipation
Proclamation in 1863,
when he declared 3.5 mil-
lion enslaved African Americans "then, thenceforward,
and forever free."

Next I went to the census data. In the 1870 census I
found them.

In 1870 "Ferrobie" was twenty-four and "keeping
house." Sharper Pegues was twenty-six and a "farm
laborer." They had three young children.

By 1880 the census listed a "Pherebia" Pegues, married
to Sharper. They now had seven children and a nephew
living with them. Their eldest daughter, Ellen, thirteen,
was already working the fields with her father, along with
their oldest son, William.

They were free, but their lives had to have been hard.
Furby died when she was forty-three, if her headstone is
more accurate than the census records. It could be that

Page No. _40_

SCHEDULE 1.—Inhabitants in _Smithville Township_, in the County of _Marlborough_, State of _S. Ca._, enumerated by me on the _27th_ day of _August_, 1870.

Post Office: _Bennettsville S.C._   _D. C. Cann_, Ass't Marshal.

In the neat handwriting of the census taker,
under Pegues Sharper, I found Furby.

neither is accurate. Still, that's older than average for an African American woman of her time. I wish I had known to look for Sharper's gravestone.

I looked in the census for further evidence of their lives. But a 1921 fire in Washington, DC, had destroyed or damaged almost all of the 1890 census.

Yet somewhere in the United States, it's likely that Furby and Sharper's great-great-great-grandchildren and beyond live on.

· · · · · · · · · ·

It was now midmorning. We moved back to the top of the hill, where we expected fainter scent because of the probable age of the burials, if they were there.

Paul let Macy search again. It was ten degrees warmer,

and Macy's behavior change was astonishing. He alerted several times, with his deep play bow. Thanks to Macy, we started to notice shapes and depressions that had been covered with leaves.

Paul pointed them out to Pat and May. The more oblong or rectangular, the more likely it was that they were burials.

Paul then ran Jordan, his other Labrador. She was soft and black, rather than hard and amber like Macy. She alerted—a paw and a light scratch—repeatedly in the deep leaves, in several spots where Macy had alerted, and

Both Jordan and Macy alerted in the same depressions.

in a couple of new places, where we then saw depressions.

I heard Solo howling. Paul turned to me once more, and I freed Solo from the car, letting him run into the little woods.

I stood well back, so that I wouldn't give away the spots. It didn't matter. Solo's work overlapped Macy's and Jordan's—several alerts and head throws in the same places. I was no longer surprised.

We finished searching for the day and placed flags at the eight spots where the dogs had consistently alerted. Pat was thrilled to have watched the dogs. The work of mapping and measuring began. Pat and I went to poke the depressions to see if we hit stone markers. They could have become buried underneath the humus of the woods. Burials of that era tended to be at least four feet deep, so it didn't feel as though we were poking at the dead.

May was happy for her friend. Pat and her family were planning to put markers there. "We don't care who is who. Now we can lay it to rest."

Solo was lying off to the side, panting, his tug toy still in his mouth. He was happy too. I hadn't put him back in the car.

The leaves where he had flung himself were disturbed. Beneath them I saw a flash of white. A tiny violet. Pat looked and then smiled.

"It's called 'spring beauty.'"

CHAPTER TWENTY-SEVEN

· · · · · · · · · ·

HILLS AND VALLEYS

It was a hot summer training night. I watched Mike Baker squeeze himself under the floor tiles in an abandoned laboratory building. Another handler slid the tiles back into place. Mike was invisible. I had claustrophobia just from watching.

Though most dogs don't have great vision, they still tend to be object-oriented. Many need to be trained to trust their noses, not their eyes, during a search. Once the less-experienced patrol dogs realized that Mike's scent was somewhere in the room, they looked behind doors. One leaped repeatedly at a large refrigerator unit because Mike's scent had crawled from underneath the floor tiles up the unit's side, and it was large enough to hold him.

Several dogs, convinced that Mike was behind a hall-way window, leaped repeatedly at the window, hoping to trigger his appearance.

Much later that night, as a group of handlers stood outside, K9 officer Danny Gooch came out after taking his turn hiding for dogs. He was sweating in a padded decoy suit. After he got help tugging the awkward suit off, he came back to the group, rolling up the sleeves of his T-shirt. He had a dark-blue tattoo of a Dutch shepherd head on his shoulder.

Another handler shook his head in mock disapproval.

Danny's white teeth flashed as he eyed the handler, whose inexperienced dog had flung himself at the glass window when Mike was hiding under the tiles.

"Hey, you know what Kimbo would have done?" Danny asked. "You know what Kimbo would have done?"

Everyone knew.

Dark little Kimbo wouldn't have been fooled. He would have smelled Mike through the small holes in the particle-board tiles, then tried to dig him out, barking ferociously.

Mike muttered to me one night, as we watched Danny and Kimbo enter a deserted cigarette factory, "If you're going into hell, that's the dog you want in front of you."

Kimbo was twelve when Danny retired him. That's old for a patrol dog, but his toughness kept him going. The last week he worked, he found a suspect's dropped gun.

The mistake of waiting too long to retire a dog can be obvious. K9 officers look with almost tender pity as a dog's back leg starts to shake when it should be solid, or a decoy gives a dog less of a swing on the bite sleeve because he's worried about hurting him.

That protective feeling can get officers injured when they need to call in a K9 on a case that involves a dangerous suspect.

Kimbo stayed at home in an increasingly customized outside kennel space. Danny's daughter, Gogo, snuck him into the house once Danny went to work.

● ● ● ● ● ● ● ● ● ● ●

Except for a smattering of gray on his muzzle and lower jaw, Solo doesn't look eight. In any case, shepherd muzzles can turn gray early in life. He doesn't act his age either.

Kimbo, a Dutch shepherd, and his handler, Danny Gooch, watch a suspect during a training exercise.

He brings us toys at night, head high, eyes gleaming. He sets them on the couch, slowly pushes them closer with his nose, and then backs away into a crouch to see if we'll take his bait.

When company arrives, he's a tiresome clown. When I tell him to lie down, he'll run at the dog bed and jump on it with his front feet, so that he can use it like a boogie board to skate across the floor, before he flips in circles and throws himself down on it with melodramatic yowls and moans.

If a particular training find poses a challenge? Once he's found the hide, he'll give himself the dog equivalent of a gold star. Or two. He does extra victory laps.

Solo aging gracefully.

Photo by D. L. Anderson

He snakes among trees and leaps over obstacles, swinging the tug toy. I stand there with my arms crossed and wait. I get it. He worked hard.

But Solo's rear left leg can wobble the day after a long training or search. His front shoulder is hinky, probably from years of leaping from the fourth stair to the concrete floor every time he comes downstairs.

One summer training at Nancy's ended with her throwing her arms up as Solo panted into an indifferent alert on a cadaver hide, tongue hanging on the grass. "Just pathetic," she declared. She looked at me accusingly.

"You really need to start another dog," she said, "if he's going to be around to teach it anything at all."

Nancy was right. Scent-detection dogs need more than their noses. If climbing a steep hill to follow scent wafting from the other side hurts too much, the dog won't go. It doesn't matter how good his nose is.

I spent the first three years of Solo's life wondering which accident, which moment of recklessness, might end his search work—running at top speed into a barbed-wire fence in the shadowy woods; hitting a glass door in an abandoned office building; dashing into the middle of a herd of cows; charging out of a warehouse and belly flopping off the loading dock.

He survived. Then we reached a plateau. Both of us were smarter. He thought before he leaped. I paid more attention to our environment.

I could speak in low sentences, or often not at all.

Unless we flushed a coyote from her den or a tiny fawn out of a swamp. Then I reminded him what the job was. I could see him switch back into work mode.

During one search a big water moccasin came thrashing out of a murky swamp toward us. I quietly called Solo away. We moved on, leaving the venomous snake in peace. It belonged there.

Those years were lovely—and temporary.

At best, Solo's got a couple of years of work left. Like me, he is headed downhill. Because he's a dog, he's moving faster than I am. Darn him. He's always been faster.

Not just joints and muscles become vulnerable. A dog's acute sense of smell doesn't last forever either. Its abilities can weaken with age, with disease, with a series of small injuries.

People's sense of smell isn't that different. As we age, it can degenerate. But the aging-nose story comes with a big exception: experience.

Perfume experts, for instance, can get better with age because they are so knowledgeable and skilled. "A given seventy-five-year-old may outperform a given twenty-five-year-old," wrote scent specialist Avery Gilbert.

Experience matters for scent-detection dogs, too. I watched several of Durham Police Department's patrol dogs who are around Solo's age. They worked with such efficiency that it wasn't until they were back in their patrol cars that I realized they had finished in half the time of the younger dogs.

Watching them work made my worries about Solo seem silly. Neither of us was ready to quit.

* * * * * * * * * *

The hard lump on Solo's front leg, just above his dewclaw, appeared a few months after I noticed a limp on that side. I called the vet. By the time Solo, David, and I arrived at her office, I'd convinced myself that Solo had bone cancer.

Shepherds get bone cancer at higher rates than most dog breeds. It shows up on the long leg bones. By the time a limp appears, the cancer has usually spread.

I told David that Solo had had a good life, an active one, and while it would be incredibly sad to lose him, it wasn't a tragedy. My chest hurt.

It wasn't the first time we'd talked about Solo having a shortened life span. He and I train and search in polluted areas. His lungs, feet, and legs have been exposed to herbicides, pesticides, and heavy metals. We've searched abandoned houses filled with chemicals and lead paint. Wrecking yards with heavy oils and antifreeze oozing into the ground. Landfills full of corrosive metals and toxic gases and liquids.

My cure-all for this exposure is simple: soap and water. First Solo, then me, as soon as we get home. Solo, who has just spent his time throwing himself with delight into muck-and-algae-filled swamps, tucks his tail and pins his ears tight against his head. Clean water terrifies him.

Is Solo more prone to cancer, or respiratory illnesses, or

getting sick from stray bacteria than a pet dog is? It's hard to know. Only a few studies address the health difference between pet dogs and working dogs. One veterinarian researcher, Cynthia Otto, studied the dogs who searched at the disaster sites after the 9/11 terrorist attacks in New York City; at the Pentagon in Washington, DC; and at the airline crash site near Shanksville, Pennsylvania.

Despite the horror of those attacks, Otto came away encouraged about one aspect: the search dogs who worked at those sites seemed to live longer, happier, and healthier lives than the average companion dog. The last surviving 9/11 search dog, a golden retriever named Bretagne, died when she was sixteen.

Perhaps, Otto thought, all the physical activity and mental stimulation search dogs get extends their lives?

If that's the case, many of us can provide something similar to our pet dogs.

• • • • • • • • • • •

Whether dogs lead active or sedate lives, cancer is common in our industrialized country. Almost half of dogs older than ten will develop cancer. Half of those will die from it.

I arrived at the vet's knowing all of this, resigned. Solo struggled briefly against the aspiration needle. He was worried the vet was going to do the unthinkable and try to trim his nails. Once he felt the thick needle piercing his skin, no big deal to him, he relaxed completely. Without

budging, he let the vet draw a core sample from the suspicious lump.

She smeared a bit of the sample onto a glass slide and
held it up to the light. She smiled.

"Grease."

It was the most wonderful word I'd ever heard. Solo
didn't have cancer. He had a bad zit.

Kent Olson and his dog, Thunder, from Lakewood, Washington,
rest briefly after searching through the rubble for victims of the
September 11 terrorist attack at the World Trade Center.

DOGGY DNA

Modern dogs aren't just people's best companions. Now they are also helping us understand human disease. How? Dogs share lots of genetic similarities with people. We also share more than four hundred diseases. That's a lot. We could start with the *A*s and go on!

- Allergies
- Anemia
- Arthritis
- Asthma

But two of the biggest diseases we share? Cancer and heart disease.

Canine genetic research is helping us spot versions of genes that make dogs more likely to get certain diseases. That means dogs may well help us understand the genetics involved in human diseases.

Good dog! Golden retrievers are one breed being closely studied for what we can learn about their genetic diseases—and potentially ours.

Not long after Solo's lump was tested, we were training off a gravel road where Durham keeps street repair
supplies. It was late summer, and night had fallen. Mike
turned his SUV around and put on its high beams. I did
the same with my car's headlights. They cast pale light
across the hills of yellow sand, gravel, and granite rubble
at the end of the road.

The limestone gravel piles went straight up fifteen or
twenty feet. The sand across from the gravel made a huge
dune, unused for so long that animals had burrowed into
it, making cave villages on the sides. The piles created
half-pipes.

Across from them lay a mound of broken granite

The pile definitely didn't look stable,
and Solo rarely trained on rubble.

curbstones. The pinkish stones looked unstable, with black gaps.

Mike had planted training material for Solo somewhere on the half-pipes of gravel and sand. Or maybe in the rubble pile.

Solo barked sharply at me, impatient to be released. I cut him free, and he disappeared into the darkness to water the trees. He came out on the back edge of the piles, running smoothly. No limp.

I didn't need to tell him to start. He motored up the sand dune, ran across the top, disappeared along the far edge, came back into the beams of the headlights, sampled the air, and then flipped himself around at the top, head raised.

He dropped in like a skateboarder on a ramp, straight down the hill, gathering steam, before switching back up and around and doing it again.

Cadaver scent from the rubble pile had clearly drifted over to the sand dune and crawled up it. Solo was so experienced that he knew what had happened. He'd used those easy swoops to reject the dune as the source of the scent. I could almost see the shape of the scent as he drew it for me.

His moves on the sand dune, as smooth as they were, worried me. I knew what came next.

I watched as he stepped up onto a slab of granite. Then again, up one more level. I stood back so that he couldn't hear any intakes of breath on my part as I watched him scale the uneven terrain.

Mike, standing behind me, said in a low voice, "I tested it." Of course he had.

Solo tested it too, moving deliberately, sticking his head into the black holes where the scent swirled.

Then, halfway up and halfway across, he froze at one hole and inhaled deeply.

He turned his head back to stare at me, eyes glowing amber in the headlights.

"Sweet," Mike said. "Sweet."

CHAPTER TWENTY-EIGHT

· · · · · · · · · · ·

PUPPY DREAMS

Solo wasn't the only aging beast in our house. All of us were getting sore and creaky. Silver crept across the tops of our heads, and in Solo's case, across his muzzle.

Megan's entire head was a mixture of white and faded mahogany, her eyes increasingly bleary, as though a fog had descended and was slowly encasing her.

She was thirteen. She was no longer as beautiful as she'd been in her youth, but she remained as self-centered and spoiled as ever and continued to demand her royal due. If Solo lay sacked out on a soft dog bed, she would totter over and collapse on top of him. She looked at him in reproach if their colliding bones startled him awake.

Her days of tearing my shoulder muscles by running out the end of her Flexi lead were gone. If she saw a squirrel, it sent her into a wobble, like a beginning gymnast on a balance beam.

Sometimes she just fell over.

We popped mild pain pills into her mouth and used an elaborate harness to help her up and down the stairs each night and morning.

We bought her a green quilted dog jacket to keep her warm. She sometimes even gazed at me with approval when I tucked a blanket over her at night. I inherited

Photo by Cat Warren

Megan was ancient in dog years, but she still ruled the roost.

Dad's cherrywood rocker, his binoculars—and Megan.

As Megan got weaker, I remembered Nancy's firm words: I needed to start another cadaver dog.

Adding another dog in the bedroom at night would ensure that it smelled like a cowboys' bunkhouse. It already sounded like one. Three of us snored occasionally.

Not Megan. Except for her sloppy drinking habits, she remained a lady, even in decline. Megan got extra food if she wanted it. No matter what she ate, she retained a wasp waist.

David promised me that as long as the three-dog days and nights didn't stretch out for years, he could put up with the unknown chaos of three generations of dogs.

. . . .

I scanned dozens of websites and hundreds of photos, raising my hopes with two-dimensional images of baby-faced German shepherd puppies. When shepherd pups are four to six weeks old, they have a flop-eared cuteness that makes anyone who loves dogs go soft and gooey inside.

By nine weeks old they look and act like clumsy sharks—all teeth and pointy snouts.

We couldn't get another Solo. I might have been tempted, but Joan Andreasen-Webb was no longer breeding shepherds. If I wanted to continue doing cadaver-dog work, my best chances lay with an entirely working-line shepherd. And I wanted to keep going.

My former fantasies of a large, calm, red-and-black

prince were gone. I had an entirely new fantasy: a sable or black shepherd with a flat back, "environmental hardness," nerve, and drive.

I knew exactly what I wanted: one of Kathy Holbert's pups from the mountains of West Virginia, raised with Kathy's laughter and working-dog knowledge; with the gentle hands of her husband, Danny; and with rollicking adventure—crawling through culverts, swimming in creeks, running through the woods, balancing on gently sloped ladders, diving into swimming pools, walking across balance beams.

Photo by Katie O'Connor

Meet Aero, a five-week-old working-line German shepherd puppy.

"You'd better have something for this pup to do once it gets to your house," Lisa Mayhew warned me. She was right. This wouldn't be a pup who was going to lie calmly, as Solo did now, snoozing while we watched television or ate dinner.

Our morning ritual of coffee in bed while reading the newspaper would be history. Solo slept in and arose, with a luxurious stretch and yawn, only when we decided to.

This would be the kind of German shepherd pup that handlers name Havoc, Harm, Hecate. Or Voldemort.

We'd kept another name in reserve for years. It had aged nicely and still rolled off our tongues with pleasurable ease: Coda.

This time I would be sobbing in David's arms late at night if the puppy *didn't* immediately leap onto us, scrabbling to pepper our arms and legs and noses and toes with puppy bites and claw marks. Solo had taught me that such behavior wasn't personal, and it wasn't aggression. It was an appetite for life.

I thought I could build in obedience, but it was harder to build drive if the basic material wasn't there. I could teach a pup not to leap over the couch and all over us and not to chew on hands.

For all our preparations and research and joy, I was scared. A puppy would take lots of time, time away from Solo. Would dog-aggressive Solo even accept a pup in the house?

And getting a new dog trained and certified can take

up to two years—if the pup continued to show promise, if the K9 teams in Durham allowed me to train with them, if no terrible accidents occurred.

I had encouragement in my forebodings. Two experienced law enforcement trainers told me that I would never again have a dog as naturally good as Solo.

When I told Nancy that, she scoffed and told me not to be melodramatic. "It's the handler, stupid," she said.

Within the hour I overheard Nancy telling a friend that she had just lied to me. I might never again have a dog as good as Solo.

"It's very common to see a dog handler be a 'one dog wonder' and to either give it up once that dog is done or to suffer miserably with the next dogs," wrote one cadaver-dog trainer.

Working-line German shepherd pups have
a well-earned nickname: "land sharks."

I was now the working-dog researcher who knew too much. Between genetics and temperament, accidents and poor health, and the limits of my ability as a still-new handler? Getting another dog to succeed felt like a crapshoot.

I had watched good handlers struggle mightily to understand and respect their new dogs—and fail. Dogs failed too. I watched almost-adult dogs get shipped in from Europe, get evaluated, and wash out. Not hitting the bite sleeve hard enough. Hesitating before leaping up a metal stairway or onto a slippery desk in a warehouse. Mike Baker, who has evaluated many hundreds of dogs, was more patient and knowledgeable than the sometimes-judgmental handlers. He knew how long the dog had been in the country, whether it had the equivalent of jet lag, what its early experience might or might not have been.

Many dogs faced entirely new environments. Breeding kennels—even top-notch European ones—can't or don't always provide pups with the exposure they need.

I would be bringing a ten-week-old puppy to K9 training who wouldn't be big enough to climb warehouse stairs.

So much could go wrong. Solo's gifts, and even his weaknesses, helped shape him and me for cadaver-dog work. There would be no beginner's luck this time around.

On the other hand, I had resources at my disposal. Nancy Hook, for example. Joan. Mike Baker promised me that, though he would be retired from the Durham K9 unit when the pup arrived, he would still be in the K9 training business and would help me put a foundation on the young dog.

During training one night, I tried to assure Mike—and myself—that I wouldn't be as clueless this time around. "I'll know more with the next one. I won't make the same mistakes."

Mike shook his head. He knew better. "If I had every dog in front of me that I'd ever worked with, I'd apologize to each of them."

· · · · · · · · · · ·

K9 handlers and I were standing outside another abandoned office building, on another hot North Carolina night. Each patrol dog had gone into the building; each dog had come out and lifted his leg on the nearby shrubbery.

The stench inspired the familiar K9 cop conversation about the superiority of male working dogs. I was used to it. The law enforcement patrol-dog world is overwhelmingly male. It creates a self-fulfilling prophecy. Any female patrol dog who managed to slip into the K9 ranks got close scrutiny until she made an error. And she would. All of us make mistakes.

I sighed and rolled my eyes as the stereotypes continued. The problem was that I too preferred male German shepherds. Solo was my third.

But I have a feminist contrary streak as well. I talked with Mike. Mike pointed out that one of the toughest dogs on the K9 team was a female. Females tended to be more focused than males, he said.

I talked with Nancy. Nancy said it depended on the dog, and I should get the pup I liked.

Joan nudged me further down the female trail. "I love the way females work," she wrote. "Totally different kind of relationship . . . at least, for me."

I thought about the cadaver and tracking dogs I had met—a mix of sexes, with just as many females as males.

Mike, Nancy, and Joan didn't tip the balance in the direction of a female. Solo put his big paw on it. He had grown up a lot in eight years. But I could easily imagine a male adolescent shepherd getting crosswise with him. And at Solo's age, I knew who would win.

One study showed that more equal relationships and play occur between male and female canines than between same-sex pairs. That made sense.

Even socially challenged Solo at times showed off for female dogs, cavorting goofily, rather than bristling. That was my hope. More romp. Fewer growls.

How, though, could I assess which female puppy to get?

Of course, I fell back on research. I found a great deal of work on "whorls"—those spots where hairs converge and then wheel one way or the other. Cowlicks. Everyone has at least one.

Australian veterinary researcher Lisa Tomkins went to town based on that work. She assessed one hundred fifteen future guide dogs, looking at both the direction of their whorls and which paw they preferred to use. Just like people tend to be left-handed or right-handed, dogs

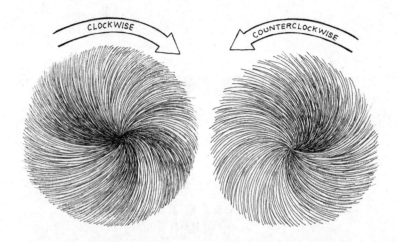

also tend to use one paw over the other. Then she followed their progress. Puppies who preferred to use their right paws over their left were twice as likely to pass guide dog school. Puppies with counterclockwise chest whorls were more than twice as likely to succeed than those with clockwise chest whorls.

I already knew Solo preferred to use his right paw to snag toys from under the couch if he couldn't use his mouth. I looked at his chest. At first all I could see was a big mass of golden fur. But as I parted the fur and moved farther down his chest, I saw one small cowlick moving in reverse.

I imagined my and David's arrival at Kathy Holbert's hilltop kennel, me with my shopping list in hand.

I'd say, "One female German shepherd puppy with a counterclockwise chest whorl and a strong right-paw preference. Along with everything else: high drive, high sociability, great health. And a sense of humor. Do you have a pup who fits that description?"

CHAPTER TWENTY-NINE

. . . .

WAG

The pups were born in early September, before the leaves of the huge sycamores started to turn yellow in the West Virginia mountains. The pups' father was such a dark sable that anyone would have called him black, though he had traces of dark velvet brown on his chest and belly. He was gorgeous.

I had already fallen for the pup's mother, Kathy's trailing and article-search dog. Reza made everything look easy. She toted around toys until she realized she was in labor. Whoops. Excuse me. Got to deliver some pups. She went back to toys soon enough, bringing them to the pups to play with. She fell into the category of "fun mom."

I watched the three female pups emerge on Facebook, via messages and photos, with Danny, Kathy's husband, holding up each one for the camera—three moles getting their first mug shot. One had a drifting trace of umbilical cord still attached. She held both pink paws up, almost as though trying to protect her homely squinty face from the camera lens. I couldn't tell if she was pushing her right paw out more than her left.

Two females were monsters right out of the womb, both more than a pound. The third female, black like one of her sisters, was half their size. Nine ounces.

Kathy named her "Little Bit."

Little Bit (left) was half the size of her littermates when she was born, but by four weeks old she'd started to catch up.

Photo by Kathy Holbert

. . . .

We assume puppies learn all sorts of things from their mothers. But do they learn by watching and then imitating, or is it instinctive? Does a foal watch his mamma drink from the creek and then mimic, or would he drink on his own? Or is it a mixture of the two?

Nancy suggested that Solo could teach the pup a thing or two. Of course, not all teaching is good teaching. Megan's belligerent barking when she sees the UPS man encourages Solo to bark as well. But Megan could simply be ramping up Solo's arousal level.

No one promised that all learning is good learning.

Scientists once thought that mimicking something after watching it being done was unique to humans. Which is weird, because we say "You're a copycat" or "Monkey see, monkey do" in a snotty tone.

But watching a person do something and then trying to do it yourself isn't easy. And being able to copy what prior generations have done is part of what makes the machinery of human culture chug along. Watch a toddler look at a dance video and then try to imitate Beyoncé's moves.

Scientists are now watching the walls between what is human and what is animal fall fast. Dogs aren't leading the experimental way, but they are part of a diverse animal pack that researchers are learning about. The crow family, meerkats, marmosets, elephants, and rats all are demonstrating what scientists once thought were uniquely human kinds of intelligence.

Not much research has been done on social learning or imitation or observational learning in working dogs, though that too is starting to change. Partly it's harder for scientists to get access to working dogs. Why? Because the dogs are working. Only one study shows what many handlers believe is the case—that working dogs learn from observing other dogs. The study used two litters of German shepherd pups. One litter got to watch their mother, a drug-detection dog, at her job. That's all they were allowed—to watch but not participate. The other litter didn't get to see their mother work.

When the pups were six months old, 85 percent of the pups who had observed their mother at work passed an

Can working pups learn from their mothers?

aptitude test for scent detection. Fewer than 20 percent of
the non-observing pups passed.

In researching, I found more good news. Dominant
animals, like Solo, are generally better teachers than sub-
missive animals.

David and I watched the videos that Kathy posted
of the four puppies—three females and a male—as they
started negotiating the PVC-pipe ladders, culverts, and
barrels she had set up for them in the play yard. We tried
not to fall in love with any pup in particular. Videos don't
tell the story; nor do photos or even e-mails. The two big
females—one black, the other black and tan and similar
to her mother in looks—showed signs of handsome adult-
hood. I avoided gazing directly at Little Bit's face. With her
wide milky-blue eyes, midnight fur, and chunky yet delicate nose, she looked like a plush Japanese anime puppy.

I also had been small and cute; people had patted me
on the head a great deal because they could. Little Bit
brought out the protective "aww" in people, not the awe I
ultimately wanted.

But she was tough. When the puppies' mother wasn't
there, one or two of them would try something, and then
another one would try.

Let's go climbing.

Let's break out of this barrel.

Let's slip and slide through this metal culvert and bite
each other.

I'm not a learning expert. All I knew, watching the

videos, was that their constant play and experimentation together—even what appeared to be occasional, perhaps accidental cooperation—meant something.

They were raggedy, impulsive, enthusiastic, distractible. Yet I saw hints of what their future might hold: an entire pack of puppies, tails wagging, diving into dense underbrush and climbing over rubble to search.

At first Little Bit couldn't climb over obstacles as easily as the larger pups. In one video Kathy chuckled quietly as five-week-old Little Bit growled in frustration and flung herself repeatedly at a broad plywood teeter-totter, a wobble board, until she finally scrabbled on, using her back feet and belly to propel herself like a turtle.

Then she ran off to play games by herself, sliding around in a big metal culvert, grabbing her own tail, going in circles inside the circle. I showed David the videos of her and told him sternly not to get attached and to look at all the strengths of the two big handsome females.

It had been easier with Solo. There hadn't been a choice.

In the end Kathy made the choice for us. She called me when the pups were eight weeks old. She had spent all day evaluating them. One of the big females I had yearned for early on was "neck and neck" with Little Bit in the hunting-for-toys tests. By the end of the day, it was clear to Kathy that Little Bit hunted longer and harder for her toy than any of the other pups.

It was behavior that one needed in a cadaver dog.

Little Bit would disappear in the dark down the road, worrying Kathy, and then come back toting a lost ball in her mouth. She found her mother's blue ball in the snow before her mother did, and grabbed it, the whites of her eyes showing against her black fur as her mother turned sideways to try to snatch it. No dice.

Little Bit was independent and contrary. She would be a pain in the butt and a joy to train. A plush toy with razor-sharp teeth and a brain.

David smiled broadly when I got off the phone. Early evaluation isn't destiny, but it helped us confirm what we already wanted: Little Bit.

Kathy told me that she and Danny had a five-minute "pity party," as Kathy called it. This pup had stubbornly squiggled her way into their hearts. Then Kathy stopped calling her Little Bit and started calling her Coda.

· · · · · · · · · · ·

We pushed hard on the toll roads, driving from West Virginia back to North Carolina to beat the setting November sun. I stewed most of the way. I was certain Solo would kill our precious sleeping cargo with one big paw and a bite. So much for Little Bit.

I went back and forth on arrangements, micromanaging the details of their meeting, dreading the tragic outcome.

We decided that I would drop David at the house. He'd exercise Solo thoroughly, and then bring him to an empty ball field a mile from the house, where Coda and I would meet them.

Megan was on an extended playdate with our good friend Barb Smalley and her dog, to keep introductions simpler.

We were punchy with exhaustion, sore, and hungry. Dusk settled in on the ball field and surrounding woods as I opened the back door of the Camry. I left Coda in her crate on the backseat. Solo leaped from the small Civic, greeted me exuberantly, and went over to sniff boulders and lift his leg. I had to call him over to the Camry. He

Coda looked a lot like a plush toy.

briefly sniffed a silent Coda through the wire grate, then returned to the more enticing dog pee on the rocks.

While he was distracted, I carried tiny Coda out onto the field, set her down, and backed up a few steps. David had Solo's red ball. I had treats. Coda barked sharply five or six times at the approaching monster, then ran back to me.

Solo sniffed her, his hackles up, tail high and wagging, then low and wagging. The hackles came down. He opened his mouth and grinned. He stretched his big body easily, luxuriously, over the black puppy, whose outline was starting to blur into the dusk.

Then he flipped toward David, who had his red ball, and levitated his back legs in a delicate move that left Coda untouched. She no longer looked cowed, but curious.

. . . .

It was that easy. Solo simply forgot that he'd spent most of his life hating other dogs. Besides, she wasn't really a dog. Not yet. She was a puppy. And she was so fascinated by everything he did. She loved to play as much as Solo. In the house. In the yard. During the day. Late at night, when our eyes drooped, and Megan slept soundly on her soft bed.

One evening we looked up to see Solo with a rope toy in his mouth. He held it at one end and trolled it back and forth slowly like a lure to entice a drowsy Coda to play. She struck like a small, fierce black trout. Once her puppy teeth hooked firmly on to the rope, Solo walked carefully, proudly, around the house. His prize, a fuzzy ball of dark fur, tail wagging madly, hung on to the other end of the tug toy.

Solo and Coda together in the house a few days after her arrival.

Photo by D. L. Anderson

NOTES AND EXTRA READING AND VIEWING FOR WHAT THE DOG KNOWS YOUNG READERS EDITION

· · · · · · · · · · ·

What the Dog Knows is partly based on my own experiences, especially since I started training and going on searches with Solo. I also watched and participated in numerous search-and-rescue seminars, cadaver-dog seminars, and police and sheriff K9 trainings and seminars. When I wasn't actively training Solo, I carried a camera, a tape recorder, and a notebook so I could be a reporter instead of a dog handler.

I interviewed dozens of people for *What the Dog Knows*: in person, on the phone, by Skype, and on e-mail. This book also depends on what are called "off-the-record" or "deep background" interviews. That means I used the material and what I learned from a particular person but didn't name them in the book or use a direct quote. Often, I knew in advance that what was said or done couldn't be used directly. Searches often involve crimes, or potential crimes, and it's important not to write about those in a way that might change a legal case's outcome. But the experiences can be written about indirectly.

Here are a few of the kinds of people I spent time with, trained with, or interviewed: dog handlers and trainers, police and sheriff deputies, search-and-rescue volunteers and managers, military personnel, forensic anthropologists, archaeologists, botanists, analytical chemists, cognitive scientists, epidemiologists (who study disease within a population of animals or people), veterinarians, conservation biologists, medical examiners, military researchers, and historians.

Several experienced trainers and handlers shared their personal archives and training and search records (if cases were fully resolved). Solo's own training and search records were incredibly helpful to me. That's why I put one of them in the book, to show how much information they contain.

I also depended on literally thousands of newspaper and magazine articles, television and radio show transcripts, academic articles and conference proceedings, military reports and studies—and several dozen books!

If I quoted someone, and what they said has quote marks around the words, those words came from extensive notes, tape-recorded conversations, e-mails, or other correspondence. In a few instances, the words were seared into my brain because I'd heard them so often or repeated them to my husband, David, and many friends. For instance, when Nancy told me the first time we met about Solo: "Stop giving him so many treats. You're making him into a wuss." Or Durham Police K9 Sergeant Mike Baker telling me that I'd make new mistakes training the next dog: "If I had every dog in front of me that I'd ever worked with, I'd apologize to each of them."

CHAPTER ONE: A FURRY PRINCE

Interviews and correspondence for this chapter include Solo's breeder, Joan Andreasen-Webb; my husband, David (who is present in every chapter in some fashion); and my own memories of growing up in Oregon, surrounded by badly behaved but beautiful Irish setters.

You can find more pictures and stories about Joan's dogs, including pictures of Solo's father, Quando, and mother, Vita, at catwarren.com/young-readers/#chap1.

To learn about singleton puppies, I depended on Patricia McConnell, one of my favorite animal behaviorists and trainers. She wrote about her experience with a single pup (also named Solo) in her 2006 book, *For the Love of a Dog: Understanding Emotion in You and Your Best Friend.* Karen London, another behaviorist and trainer who works with aggression in dogs, wrote a piece for *Bark* magazine in December 2012 on singletons that helps explain their unique problems: catwarren.com /young-readers/#chap1.

Schutzhund is a sport designed to help people know which dogs might be the most obedient and courageous. It has three parts to it: obedience, tracking, and protection work. While it was originally designed for German shepherds, these days you can see many other herding and working breeds competing on the field, including Dobermans, Rottweilers, giant schnauzers, Belgian Malinois, boxers, and Dutch shepherds. This video shows some of the difficult things dogs learn to do in Schutzhund: catwarren.com/young-readers/#chap1.

The history of the German shepherd is complicated. They were first used for herding and guarding sheep in the nineteenth century, but they didn't look much like German shepherds you are likely to see today. In 1899 a German military officer, Max von Stephanitz, bought a dog he named Horand von Garath. That dog, who slightly resembled a wolf, was the

ancestor of the modern German shepherd: catwarren.com
/young-readers/#chap1.

CHAPTER TWO: THE BRAT KING

I corresponded with Joan constantly for this chapter. She sent me
dozens of pictures of Solo as a puppy, often taken by her friend,
Sherri Clendenin. She told me how Solo's mother, the young and
lively Vita, treated him. I loved her description of Solo's great-
aunt Cora helping raise him. Nine months before Solo was born,
David and I visited Joan and her husband, Peter, in Ohio. We met
Cora, Vita—and Solo's father, Quando. Vita was lightning fast.
Cora carted around a wastepaper basket, wagging her tail. And
Quando lay his head against my leg, and I fell in love with him.

Learning about the dog's nose, or any animal's nose, isn't
easy. Scientists learn more every day about how both dogs—and
humans—are able to smell even very faint odors: catwarren.com
/young-readers/#chap2. If you want to learn more about dogs'
senses, not just their noses, you might read Alexandra Horowitz's 2016 *Inside of a Dog: What Dogs See, Smell, and Know—
Young Readers Edition*. And if you want to try some interesting
scent and sense experiments with your dog or a friend's dog, the
2018 book *Dog Science Unleashed: Fun Activities to Do with
Your Canine Companion*, by Jodi Wheeler-Toppen, is great.

Solo isn't related, except very distantly, to African wild
dogs. But that species is considered one of the most social of
all the canids (a group that includes wolves, foxes, coyotes,
jackals, and dogs). Here, you can read more about wild dogs
and listen to their amazing language. Sometimes, they sound
like birds or squirrels, chittering and chattering when they
talk with one another: catwarren.com/young-readers/#chap2.

CHAPTER THREE: THE LANGUAGE OF OUCH

William G. Syrotuck's book, *Scent and the Scenting Dog*, first published in 1972, has long been considered the classic text on tracking and trailing. And *Bark* magazine has a nice overview on scent tracking with your dog from 2008, updated in February 2015: catwarren.com/young-readers/#chap3.

Interactive maps can provide wonderful information. This 2011 *New York Times* map shows where to live to avoid natural disasters. I saw here how very safe Corvallis, Oregon, was from natural disasters: catwarren.com/young-readers/#chap3. But you can find interactive maps for almost anything. National Geographic has a cool mapping tool online where you can make your own interactive map, adding layers that show everything from the range of the gray wolf to sea surface temperatures: catwarren.com/young-readers/#chap3.

CHAPTER FOUR: HOW TO TRAIN YOUR TASMANIAN DEVIL

This chapter partly depends on interviews and conversations I had with Nancy Hook about Solo, search-and-rescue work, and cadaver-dog work. But then I started learning about the beginning of dogs and people, many thousands of years ago. That meant reading science and history journals, and also studying how ancient religions treated dogs.

You can see more pictures of Nancy's training center, some of the scent-detection dogs she has worked with (including Solo), and see her grandson Sean training dogs: catwarren.com/young-readers/#chap4.

Search-and-rescue dog training is complicated. You can

learn more about the different search specialties, including cadaver dogs, from this 2002 *National Geographic* article: catwarren.com/young-readers/#chap4.

We are still trying to learn how far back dogs and humans go. We don't have the full story yet, and perhaps we never will. The dog skulls found in the Czech Republic were some of the oldest ever found. One famous evolutionary scientist, Greger Larson, told a reporter: "We're going to get a lot more confused before we figure out what's really going on." This *Discover* magazine piece from November 2016 asks a good question, "When Did Rover Come on Over?": catwarren.com/young-readers/#chap4.

Whether Egypt's god Anubis is a desert dog, a jackal, a golden wolf, or a mix of these remains unknown. You can watch a video about the incredibly complex (and yes, a little scary) god: catwarren.com/young-readers/#chap4.

The sidebar "Our Oldest Best Friend?" depends on many sources. In 2017 archaeologists discovered cliffside rock art with hundreds of hunting-scene pictures. They can't precisely date the art, but the pictures may be more than eight thousand years old! Here is a good article in *Science* magazine about the discovery: catwarren.com/young-readers/#chap4.

CHAPTER FIVE: THE WHOLE TOOTH

Solo learned to hunt for the particular scent of human remains using buckets in Nancy's yard, but here's another system: a daisy wheel. In this video, a young Labrador retriever works on scent wheels. When he finds the odor he gets a food reward for, watch how he freezes and then starts to drool: catwarren.com/young-readers/#chap5.

I wrote about a similar kind of foundation training with

Jaco, one of our sweet German shepherds, for *Bark* magazine in September 2016: catwarren.com/young-readers/#chap5.

Dog-book writer and journalist Maria Goodavage wrote about dogs' noses for *Dogster* magazine in June 2018: catwarren .com/young-readers/#chap5.

Dogs can be trained to sniff out almost anything! I think one of the most fascinating things well-trained scent detection dogs can find is the scat, or poop, of endangered or threatened species. Conservation Canines, based at the University of Washington, works across the globe now—finding everything from killer whales to Pacific pocket mice: catwarren.com /young-readers/#chap5.

CHAPTER SIX: THE MAGICIAN

Kevin George was talented and beloved—especially by the young, bored "mall rats" he befriended, but also by handlers and dogs everywhere. He was one of the funniest storytellers I've ever met. A group of us laughed so hard at one of his long shaggy dog stories about a patrol K9 in a department store that we were holding our sides, tears running down our faces! This appreciation of Kevin's life, "Dog Trainer, ju-jitsu master, rodeo clown," shows what a complicated and interesting man he was: catwarren.com/young-readers/#chap6.

This video explains how three-cup shuffle, or three-card monte, gets people to bet more and more money: catwarren .com/young-readers/#chap6.

Here's the full citation for the article that inspired the sidebar "Our Shrewd Ancestors": "Fossil Evidence on Origin of the Mammalian Brain," by Timothy B. Rowe, Thomas E. Macrini, and Zhe-Xi Luo, *Science* 332 (2011): 955–957. See if you can find the summary of the article online. Academic journal articles can be hard to read because they are filled with specialized language. This press release from May 2011 gives the highlights: catwarren.com/young-readers/#chap6.

CHAPTER SEVEN: A FISH PIPE AND A HANDBOOK

This chapter was fun to write because I got to visit and interview people I respect a lot. Nancy Hook, of course. I flew to Seattle to meet Andy Rebmann and his wife, Marcia Koenig, who is also an experienced trainer and handler. Andy has done thousands of searches, for both live and dead people. He is a founder of cadaver-dog work.

The book *Cadaver Dog Handbook: Forensic Training and Tactics for the Recovery of Human Remains* by Andrew Rebmann, Edward David, and Marcella H. Sorg sits on my shelf at home, and I still dip into it! So can you, by using Amazon's feature called "Look Inside": catwarren.com/young-readers/#chap7.

You can read about and see pictures of Andy and Marcia and their many scent-detection dogs working at disaster scenes and on missing person cases on my website: catwarren.com/young-readers/#chap7.

What are dogs smelling when they smell human death? It is so complicated, but this 2016 *Scienceline* article starts to explain what *odor mortis*, or smell of death, might be: catwarren.com/young-readers/#chap7.

CHAPTER EIGHT: SEESAWS

This was a hard chapter for me because I wrote about losing my father. He was a wonderful man, and I still miss him. I have so many good memories of him, though. He taught me to fish, to garden, to read, to enjoy the natural world around me. So most days, instead of feeling sad, I feel glad I had him in my life for so many years.

Nancy helped me figure out how to teach Solo all the things he needed to know. Training your dog to be a search-and-rescue dog, or a cadaver dog, goes beyond that dog being able to recognize scent! Here's a great article on DogAppy from February 2018 that explains a few of the things a search dog needs to learn: catwarren.com/young-readers/#chap8.

CHAPTER NINE: CAROLINA COW PIES

Patricia McConnell helped me understand how complicated dog aggression is. She is an ethologist, someone who studies animal behavior. She specializes in behavior problems in dogs, especially fear and aggression. She worked with one of her own border collies, Will, on this very issue. Here is a blog post by scientist Julie Hecht about Patricia's 2017 book, *The Education of Will*: catwarren.com/young-readers/#chap9.

I used a training record model from *Cadaver Dog Handbook* for Solo. But there are lots of models out there. The hundreds of records I wrote training Solo helped me write this book! Training records are important if you have to testify in court about a case. You can produce your records, showing exactly what problems you trained your dog on.

This great website lists 646 insects that can be found in North Carolina: catwarren.com/young-readers/#chap9. Sometimes, when I trained Solo with Nancy, she was also working with handlers who had search-and-rescue dogs. I'd lay a track for one of them but take a field guide along with me, as I had to hide in a field or woods for a dog to find me. I might wait up to half an hour. But I never got bored because I could sit, look around, and identify the trees, bugs, and birds that surrounded me.

CHAPTER TEN: LIBERTY WAREHOUSE

Here's an article from the *BBC News Magazine* in February 2014 about "napoo" and other slang words used in World War I: catwarren.com/young-readers/#chap10.

The Bone Room, originally located in the Bay Area in California, is a fascinating place that sells animal bones, curiosities, insects, meteorites—and human bones: catwarren.com/young -readers/#chap10.

Here's a beautiful photo of the front of Liberty warehouse before it was mostly torn down in 2014 to build luxury high-rise apartments. Developers kept just the facade to make it appear "historic": catwarren.com/young-readers/#chap10.

CHAPTER ELEVEN: AN ANCHOR ON A LEASH

This chapter is mostly about meeting Sergeant Mike Baker, the Durham Police Department K9 unit, and my early training with Mike. But I also spent several days in Florida watching young dogs and handlers work under the watchful, expert eye of law enforcement K9 trainer Steve Sprouse: catwarren.com/young -readers/#chap11.

Since 2006 I've been able to observe police K9 handlers and dogs learn and work together. Here's a 2013 article that ran in a North Carolina newspaper about training with Mike Baker: catwarren.com/young-readers/#chap11.

What law enforcement canines do during the day and night really depends on the city or town they work in. But here is a 2017 article from the American Kennel Club that gives an over-

view of the range of activities a police K9 might do: catwarren
.com/young-readers/#chap11.

CHAPTER TWELVE:
GOLDILOCKS AND THE THIRTEEN BEASTS

The history of training dogs and other animals for scent detection in the 1960s and 1970s is complicated. Different agencies were doing different things. The only thing that people generally agreed on? Dogs, properly bred and trained, were invaluable!

Here's a good biography of Tom Slick Jr. and the Southwest Research Institute he founded: catwarren.com/young -readers/#chap12.

A sentry-dog handler who worked with a German shepherd, Smokey, in Vietnam wrote this long *New York Times* opinion piece in 2017 about military dogs during that conflict: catwarren .com/young-readers/#chap12.

Here is a link to download the original study about all the animals that the Southwest Research Institute tried to train. The researchers named the animals. Greta the pig. Wiley the coyote. Sherlock the silver fox: catwarren.com/young -readers/#chap12.

CHAPTER THIRTEEN: THE SWAMP

I was able to interview the K9 handler whose dog almost drowned looking for the victim in this chapter and the next one. I had news articles as well about the victim. I went back, several years later, to the same spot Solo and I searched with a botanist, Wade Wall, who gave me a tour of the plants and soil there. Two field guides that focus on North Carolina plants and flowers were especially helpful!

Ticks carry tons of diseases, and those diseases are on the rise across the country, not just in North Carolina. Here's a handy song by Wood Newton about what to do after you've been outside where ticks are active: catwarren.com/young-readers/#chap13.

CHAPTER FOURTEEN: A SERIOUS GAME

The wetlands of North Carolina are wonderful and varied. Even though Solo and I were searching in a polluted area, wildlife and plant life are plentiful there. This site features all the different kinds of swamps and wetlands throughout North Carolina and the plant, bird, and animal species you might find there: catwarren.com/young-readers/#chap14.

PLS, or Point Last Seen, is only one of many acronyms, or abbreviations, used in the search world. Here's a handy glossary of other abbreviations and terms search experts use: catwarren .com/young-readers/#chap14.

The *New York Times* ran an article in December 2015 about how poison ivy is changing because of climate change: catwarren .com/young-readers/#chap14.

CHAPTER FIFTEEN: GRAINS OF SAND

This chapter is based on my own search experience, my own background working for and with newspapers, television, and radio, and personal conversations and interviews with other cadaver-dog handlers and trainers, detectives, and forensic anthropologists. I also trained Solo and other dogs at a research facility that studies how people decompose in various scenarios in the woods. Generous people donate their bodies, and researchers and law enforcement—and cadaver-dog teams—can learn so much from them.

While some people are grossed out by turkey vultures, I've grown to admire them! You can learn more about these fascinating birds from the Cornell Lab of Ornithology and even listen to the weird hiss they make when they are irritated: catwarren .com/young-readers/#chap15.

Weather maps, installed on your phone as an app, are crucial in tracking current and even past weather during training and searches. I like one called the Weather Underground (wunderground.com) because I can easily see incoming thunderstorms, get exact wind conditions and humidity, and find information about weather in a location over the past days, weeks, and even months. But there are all sorts of weather apps out there.

Alzheimer's and other forms of dementia are sad conditions. Search experts know that finding someone who suffers from severe memory loss demands a different set of skills. In May 2010 the *New York Times* wrote about it: catwarren.com /young-readers/#chap15.

CHAPTER SIXTEEN: MOUSE JUICE

I spent lots of time with Suzie and Roy Ferguson for this chapter, which was a great deal of fun. I first met them at the February 2011 National Search Dog Alliance seminar in Eatonton, Georgia. But I also visited them in their home close to the Great Smoky Mountains in Tennessee and got to observe a weekend training with their Tennessee search-and-rescue team. The National Search Dog Alliance also has seminars and tests for dog-and-handler certification across the country: catwarren .com/young-readers/#chap16. The Tennessee Special Response Team-A that Roy and Suzie Ferguson are members of has a webpage that you can access from my website. It isn't fancy, but it's highly functional! catwarren.com/young-readers/#chap16.

Here is a June 2018 article about a large-scale search-and-rescue scenario in eastern Oregon. It explains how important scenarios are. Everyone needs practice so that they can be fast and effective when something happens in real life: catwarren.com/young-readers/#chap16.

CHAPTER SEVENTEEN: THE ZOMBIE HANDLER

I attended the October 2011 National Network of Canine Detection Services Working Dog Seminar in Holly Springs, Mississippi, for part of this chapter. That's when I met Haylee. I had already met Lisa Higgins, her grandmother, months before at the February seminar where I met Roy and Suzie. And then, just a month after that, I went to the November 2011 Cadaver Dog Workshop at Western Carolina University, where I met Brad Dennis. That was a busy year!

Here you can find the website for the search organization that Lisa Higgins founded. Haylee was a junior member of this team: catwarren.com/young-readers/#chap17.

Brad Dennis is the national search director for the Klaas-Kids Foundation and has managed search efforts across the country for missing or abducted children for thirty years. I don't know anyone who knows more about the subject. He's dedicated and passionate—and has saved many lives with his work, as well as helped families find resolution.

CHAPTER EIGHTEEN: DOG TALES AND HORSE HOOEY

Here's a nice 2015 story from *Science* magazine about why and how dogs stole our hearts. catwarren.com/young-readers/#chap18.

Here's a great article by scent-work trainer Stacy Barnett

about false alerts in the sport of nosework: catwarren.com
/young-readers/#chap18.

If you want to read more about Clever Hans, who managed
to stump a lot of clever people, you can read about him, his
owner, the people who contributed to his reputation—and those
who helped debunk it—on the Mysteries and Science website:
catwarren.com/young-readers/#chap18.

CHAPTER NINETEEN: CLEVER HANS IN THE COURTROOM

I interviewed a number of people for this chapter. It's hard for
people who really love and respect scent-detection dogs to watch
people lie about them, and to see how much harm can be done.

The *New York Times* wrote about Keith Pikett and his dogs in
November 2011 as cases he was involved in started to fall apart:
catwarren.com/young-readers/#chap19.

Here is an explanation of how blind and double-blind studies work in science: catwarren.com/young-readers/#chap19.
The same principles hold true for dog training.

CHAPTER TWENTY: E-NOSE

I didn't assume, in writing this chapter, that the dog-versus-
machine battle was automatically going to come out with dogs
on top. News coverage comes out almost every month about a
new invention, and the claims are always similar. Here's one
story from June of 2018: "The results were good news for the
research team. But they might not be such good news for our
four-legged friends, who could soon be out of a job": catwarren
.com/young-readers/#chap20.

This interesting December 2016 article from CBC Radio

One in Canada shows both why a good nose rocks, and how truly understanding how dogs' noses work might be a fine way to start building a better artificial nose: catwarren.com /young-readers/#chap20.

CHAPTER TWENTY-ONE: THE MONSTER MASH

I love finding interesting old research papers in tiny corners of the Web. For me, it's like a scavenger hunt. That's how I found the "insect ambush detector" study. You can download and read it: catwarren.com/young-readers/#chap21.

Hate spinach? Well, scientists probably prefer you don't eat this bionic spinach—it signals to a cell phone that explosives are nearby. Could it still send a signal from your stomach if you ate it? *Forbes* magazine wrote about the research in October 2016: catwarren.com/young-readers/#chap21.

If you want to read more about Sherlock the vulture and his "friends"—and see a picture of him with his trainer, German Alonso—the *Independent*, a United Kingdom newspaper, wrote about them in July 2011: catwarren.com/young-readers/#chap21.

CHAPTER TWENTY-TWO: BOSS OF THE BOAT

I interviewed lots of people for this chapter and watched dogs and handlers work on water at several seminars and sheriff K9 trainings. And of course, I watched Solo!

A talented handler and trainer in Canada, Kim Cooper, is featured in this long CBC Radio article about cadaver dogs helping pinpoint a drowning victim: catwarren.com/young -readers/#chap22.

Marcia Koenig has done hundreds of searches with her

dogs, and one of her specialties is searching on water. You can read more about her and her current search dog, Raven, here: catwarren.com/young-readers/#chap22.

CHAPTER TWENTY-THREE: THE DOGS OF PEACE

Interviews and correspondence for this chapter included University of Rhode Island professor and documentary filmmaker Mary Healey Jamiel; Andy Rebmann; retired Rhode Island State Trooper Matt Zarrella; and a number of personal communications with handlers, trainers, and military working-dog handlers.

Theo. F. Jager's 1917 book, *Scout, Red Cross and Army Dogs: A Historical Sketch of Dogs in the Great War and a Training Guide for the Rank and File of the United States Army* can be accessed here: catwarren.com/young-readers/#chap23. World War I is still called "The Great War," but there was nothing great about it, except that it was huge, it spread across the world, and forty million people either died or were wounded.

This November 2013 story from the BBC shows how dogs were used in World War I. It's hard to find accurate stories, but this one depends on old newspaper photos: catwarren.com /young-readers/#chap23.

Here's a nice video and story from NBC News in December 2013 about Matt Zarrella. He and his first search dog found a lost, shivering teenager the first time they were called out: catwarren.com/young-readers/#chap23. Ultimately, filmmaker Mary Healey Jamiel made a documentary about Matt titled "Searchdog": catwarren.com/young-readers/#chap23.

This chapter is about American military people still missing in action, but in Vietnam, families also think about their missing. Here's a 2018 project from the Pulitzer Center about the 300,000 Vietnamese MIAs (missing in action) that families in Vietnam still wonder about and mourn: catwarren.com/young -readers/#chap23.

CHAPTER TWENTY-FOUR: WATER WITCH

This was a difficult chapter to write. It was very sad and hard to report. In conflicts and war, information can be scarce and often wrong. There is a nineteenth-century turn of phrase that captures the uncertainty: "the fog of war." I interviewed several people: Kathy Holbert, of course, but others involved with dogs working in Iraq and Afghanistan. I had access to a PowerPoint presentation of the recovery that included photographs of Strega working on the river. I also depended on articles from the Associated Press, the BBC, and many military news accounts and pictures.

Here is a gallery of military photographs showing Kathy Holbert, along with two other handlers, training their cadaver dogs in Iraq: catwarren.com/young-readers/#chap24.

This is a beautiful and sometimes harrowing series of photos from the June 2014 *Atlantic* magazine. It also shows K9s and handlers working in Iraq and Afghanistan: catwarren.com /young-readers/#chap24.

If you look at this satellite Google Map of the long Murghab River, you can see how much people depend on water for life. Zoom out, and you can see how much arid desert surrounds the river. Zoom in, and you can see the farms and crops (although not the humans and animals) dependent on the river: catwarren .com/young-readers/#chap24.

CHAPTER TWENTY-FIVE: ON WOLF STREET

If it's hard to report on current or recent conflicts, it can be even more difficult to capture the truth of what happened during the Civil War in our own country. But the story of what happened in Thomasville, Georgia, drew me in and took me deep into soldiers' diaries and the history of Andersonville Prison. Sometimes, small stories help illustrate big pictures.

Lessel Long was a Union soldier, and a prisoner of war at Andersonville—and at Thomasville. You can read his diary, published in 1886. Its title is long: *Twelve Months in Andersonville: On the March—in the Battle—in the Rebel Prison Pens, and at Last in God's Country*: catwarren.com/young-readers/#chap25. It's important to remember that a diary represents the memories of only one person.

The National Park Service wrote an in-depth article on one of the more recent searches at Thomasville where both cadaver dogs and FBI trainees participated: catwarren.com/young -readers/#chap25.

CHAPTER TWENTY-SIX: THE BURIAL GROUNDS

This chapter on searching for historic human remains in South Carolina depended on numerous online ancestry records, census records, and family letters and stories. Pat Franklin, May Mac-Callum, and Paul Martin were extremely helpful. I also was able to pull up census records and even Pegues family wills on the Web. The saddest thing about researching and writing this chapter was imagining the hard lives of the slaves and realizing their histories were barely visible compared with those of the white plantation owners.

Here's a video from Fox 28 Media from January 2019 on Paul Martin and a quick overview of the advantage of using dogs to help detect historic remains: catwarren.com/young-readers/#chap26.

"The Swamp Fox," Francis Marion, was a fascinating and crafty man. But many legends and portraits of him distort the truth. *Smithsonian* magazine wrote a history of Marion in June 2007 that gives a more accurate picture: catwarren.com/young -readers/#chap26.

CHAPTER TWENTY-SEVEN: HILLS AND VALLEYS

Dogs get old, get diseases, slow down. Working dogs retire, just like people. But one of the nice things I learned working on this chapter is that lots of working dogs live long, happy lives. And that scientists and medical researchers are finding that studying dogs and their health is also helping people.

Bretagne, a golden retriever, was the last surviving search dog from the 9/11 disaster. She died just one month shy of her seventeenth birthday. That's a great old age for any dog. Here's a piece about her and her handler on NBC's *Today* show in 2016: catwarren.com/young-readers/#chap27.

Nature magazine is one of the top science research journals in the country. When scientific breakthroughs occur, it's often *Nature* that publishes them. This November 2018 piece explains how important understanding cancer in dogs is to understanding cancer in humans—and even finding treatments for both humans and dogs: catwarren.com/young-readers/#chap27.

CHAPTER TWENTY-EIGHT: PUPPY DREAMS

You can access a link to see shots of Kathy Holbert's German shepherds on my website: catwarren.com/young-readers/#chap28.

Patricia McConnell wrote in 2009 and again in 2017 about the differences between male and female dogs for *Bark* magazine. Guess what? Everyone had a different opinion! catwarren .com/young-readers/#chap28.

Some explanation of Tomkins's interesting work can be viewed on the archives of the 2012 *Catalyst* show of Australia's ABC, "Left Paw Right Paw": catwarren.com/young-readers/#chap28.

CHAPTER TWENTY-NINE: WAG

Imitation in humans and animals is a field filled with interesting results. Here is a July 2017 article in *Cosmos* about a study of imitation in children and bonobo apes. Children imitate for no apparent reason! catwarren.com/young-readers/#chap29.

Research on bird intelligence is taking flight. It's very hard to prove abilities such as animals planning in advance the way humans can. But these rooks who clean up people's messes are very smart birds: catwarren.com/young-readers/#chap29.

ACKNOWLEDGMENTS

• • • • • • • • • • •

This is a book about a dog. But it's also about other dogs. And people. First, though, I have to thank Solo.

He wouldn't care about being acknowledged, but he is the reason for this book. I first decided to write *What the Dog Knows* because I wanted to remember him and what he taught me. My universe expanded hugely because of him. It keeps on expanding. Just as our universe is doing.

I've learned from the dogs who came before Solo—Tarn, Zev, and yes, flighty Megan! And from the dogs who came after—Coda, Jaco, and Rev. Each dog teaches me different things. And each time I think I know something about dogs, they humble me. Right now, our new German shepherd pup, Rev, is teaching me how to take each day and savor it.

Over the past years since I started this project, many different people helped me create *What the Dog Knows* and now its *Young Readers Edition*: dog people, scientists, law enforcement people, medical examiners, editors and publishers and photographers and publicists, and close friends and colleagues.

I want to thank the young readers who helped me realize that I could make my original book into something more appealing to them. Here are only a few of the children and young adults who played a role in making this a better book: Haylee Carney, whose love of scent-detection dogs and life is an inspiration. Ronnie Martin, Paul's son, whose enthusiasm for the original *What the Dog Knows* and reading about his father's work with cadaver dogs made me realize I should do this version. Lincoln Bryant, who made thoughtful comments throughout the original version of the book—what he liked, what he loved, and what bored him! Lincoln helped me think long and hard about what worked and what didn't work in the original book. I treasure some of the wry notes he made. Isaac Trost did the same thing with a markup pen and his own wise perspective. Erin Taylor, whose aunt, Lisa Mayhew, is throughout this book and my life, provided great editorial comment. Maggie Hayward also provided unique, thoughtful comments. Then there's the Shipman girls. Who rock. And whose enthusiasm for dogs and for life is boundless.

Next, I want to acknowledge a group of people I cannot name because they are linked to cases: the dedicated, patient, knowledgeable, and brave members of law enforcement and search specialists across North Carolina, the ones willing to go down in the swamp, to bushwhack, to think through all the possibilities. The work they do is hard, and I cannot thank them enough—for the safety they provide, for the care they bring to their work, and for what they have taught me.

Then come the dog people: Joan Andreasen-Webb, Nancy Hook, and Mike Baker. Joan, Solo's breeder, taught me about German shepherds for the first time in my life. Her patience and kindness and deep knowledge of dogs, especially the German shepherd, continue to inspire me. Nancy, Solo's and my first trainer, rearranged my life, just as Solo did, and gave me a new way to be with dogs. And I have been enormously lucky to train with Mike. His enormous talent, his deep knowledge of dogs, his quiet authority, his unending patience, and his ability to make dog work into dog play inspire me.

Many other North Carolina law enforcement K9 trainers and handlers tolerated me and sometimes welcomed me, helped me train Solo and the dogs who came after Solo, and let me learn by watching them. I also learned at law enforcement K9 seminars and conferences, where I got to take notes and photos, and also train Solo!

A special thanks goes to Andy Rebmann and Marcia Koenig. At the same seminar where I joined Andy and Marcia, I was able to spend time with Kevin George, one of the most talented and imaginative trainers I've ever met. At cadaver-dog seminars in Georgia, Mississippi, Louisiana, and North Carolina, I was able to observe and train with Lisa Higgins, one of the best teachers and mentors I've ever had. Now-retired Broward sheriff patrol K9 trainer Steve Sprouse welcomed me into his training seminars in both Florida and North Carolina. Although he doesn't directly appear in this young readers edition, he influenced it.

This book also depended greatly on many scientists, medical examiners, epidemiologists, veterinarians, dog behaviorists, archaeologists, anthropologists, historians, amateur historians, military personnel, and environmental scientists who were unstinting in their willingness to e-mail, talk, and fact-check.

Belle Boggs, who taught elementary school and high school, and now teaches at NC State with an office close to mine,